The Silent Musician

The Silent Musician

Why Conducting Matters

MARK WIGGLESWORTH

THE UNIVERSITY OF CHICAGO PRESS

The University of Chicago Press, Chicago 60637
© 2018 by Mark Wigglesworth
All rights reserved. No part of this book may be used or reproduced in any
manner whatsoever without written permission, except in the case of brief
quotations in critical articles and reviews. For more information, contact
the University of Chicago Press, 1427 E. 60th St., Chicago, IL 60637.
Published 2019
Printed in the United States of America

28 27 26 25 24 23 22 21 20 19   1 2 3 4 5

ISBN-13: 978-0-226-62255-2 (CLOTH)
ISBN-13: 978-0-226-62269-9 (E-BOOK)
DOI: https://doi.org/10.7208/chicago/9780226622699.001.0001

First published by Faber & Faber, Ltd., 2018.

LIBRARY OF CONGRESS CATALOGING-IN-PUBLICATION DATA
Names: Wigglesworth, Mark, 1964– author.
Title: The silent musician : why conducting matters / Mark Wigglesworth.
Description: Chicago : The University of Chicago Press, 2019.
Identifiers: LCCN 2018042648 | ISBN 9780226622552 (cloth : alk. paper)
| ISBN 9780226622699 (ebook)
Subjects: LCSH: Conducting.
Classification: LCC ML458 .W54 2019 | DDC 781.45—dc23
LC record available at https://lccn.loc.gov/2018042648

♾ This paper meets the requirements of ANSI/NISO Z39.48-1992
(Permanence of Paper).

for Annemieke,
who understands what a conductor does,

and for Clara,
who one day might like to know too.

Contents

Time.

There is no force more powerful.

It waits for no one, cares for nothing.

We cannot control it. We cannot influence it. We can never be free from its irrevocable journey, nor deny its relentless passage. Sometimes even clocks do not keep up with it.

But we can control our perception of time.

Through music we can experience an hour as if it were a minute or a minute as if it were an hour. Music gives us the power to live in the present. There is no past on which to reflect. No future on which to dream. Music releases the present from the weight of its past and the expectations of its future. Such separation can bring profound relief.

All musicians have the privilege of playing with time. But for conductors time is our most significant responsibility, weaving pulses in and out of its unwavering path, generating a more forgiving vision of its inevitable tread. We seek to organise music within time while simultaneously releasing it from the restrictions time imposes. We work within the boundaries of this paradox, managing the ebb and flow of music to defy a ticking clock and inspire a pulsing heart.

We beat time.

We shape the invisible.

Shaping the Invisible

Music is the art of sounds in the movement of time.
Ferruccio Busoni

A conductor is one of classical music's most recognisable figures. Many people who have never been to an orchestral concert will have an image of what one looks like. Yet even for music lovers the role can be a dubious one, mysterious at best. The confusion is understandable. Within a context that is essentially only about sound, there is something surprising about the significance given to someone who remains completely silent. It is intriguing that an art form that is not supposed to be about what you see should so often be embodied by someone you cannot hear.

The comic stereotype of an indulged megalomaniac, whose self-importance doesn't seem to match what the orchestra musicians are doing, is a pervasive cliché. The last person to enter the room, apparently possessed of a paranormal ability to determine precisely when the atmosphere is conducive to begin, proceeds to perform a series of exaggerated gestures that vaguely coincide with the energy of the music, conjuring up a cauldron of magical sounds with a wand-like stick, subsequently accepting the ensuing applause while simultaneously acknowledging with self-proclaimed humility and sheepish demur both the music and the people who played it, exiting the stage with a profound tread that informs us exactly how much we have all been moved by the power of the breathtaking experience we have shared. It's easy to laugh at people who take themselves so seriously, especially if we think their work might be completely irrelevant.

However, I don't think the profession would exist if it was unnecessary. In fact, conductors are in a position to influence the musical lives of many classical music lovers, both in the orchestra and in the audience, to a significant degree. Whether we do or not, of course, depends on how good we are at our job.

Rarely does such a well-known profession attract so many questions: 'Surely orchestras can play perfectly well without you?' 'Do you really make any difference to the performance?' 'Are the musicians actually watching you?' Some of these even come from orchestra players themselves! Yet though any human relationship is based on untold complex, subconscious, and often inexplicable forces, and the dynamic between an individual and a group is rarely simple, the role of a conductor – I believe – is no great mystery.

People wonder less about leadership in other occupations. I doubt if many theatre directors, sports coaches, or frankly anyone whose success depends on an ability to empower others, generate quite as much puzzlement. Is it the greater familiarity with drama, sport, or business that makes it easier to appreciate why a cast of actors has someone in charge, why eleven individuals don't necessarily make a team, or why companies profit from being inspired by someone who is free to focus on the overview? A good conductor unifies and inspires a large group of people for exactly the same set of reasons that any other leader does. Retaining one's own responsibility for decision-making while creating a rewarding collective sense of collaboration might not be an exact science, but few would disagree that such a combination is the goal of contemporary leadership in pretty much any field.

A conductor is one of the few people whose authority is exercised in public. Although you would think that the highly visible nature of the role might make it easier to understand than the work of someone behind the scenes, the opposite seems to be the case. It is clearly the sight of the conductor that creates the confusion. Conductors are more hands on than most leaders. The complication is that the language we use is figurative, and our mode of communication can appear questionable to an audience that is probably not meant to see it at work at all. It's hard for the public in a concert hall to avoid observing the physicality of a conductor, but our gestures are no more a means to an end than is an instrumentalist's fingering. I'm not sure it should matter to the listener what a conductor looks like – yet everything about the visual mechanics of a live orchestral concert seems to suggest that it does.

A three-year-old I used to know always referred to me as 'The Connector'. Like many malapropisms, her delightful slip of the tongue reveals a lot. Conducting is all about connecting. You try to connect the composer to the musicians to the music to the audience, and hope that by strengthening these links you are a conductor in the scientific sense of the term – a body that transmits heat, electricity, or sound. And away from a scientific context, the most common non-musical meaning of the verb 'to conduct' is well understood. An usher conducting you to your seat will most likely walk alongside you, probably just a shade in front, but as much accompanying you as leading you. And the amount of guidance you receive will depend as much on you as on the person who is conducting you. The usher is undoubtedly in charge, but not by much. 'Leading with' is an etymological as well as a musical definition of conducting, for though musical performances must have a clear sense of direction, an orchestra is a body of musicians that needs to be empowered to express itself. Managing a broad coalition that still has a distinct vision as its aim might appear a contradiction to some, but the best conductors achieve precisely this combination without any artistic compromise. Good leaders don't just shout commands and expect them to be followed, and successful teams in any environment are as much about the individuality of its members as they are about discipline. This is particularly true for an orchestra whose players have to be able to take ownership of the performance if it is to sound credible to those who are listening.

My earliest memory of a conductor is a televised performance of Mahler's gigantic Eighth Symphony. I watched the first few bars, went off to play outside, and returned just in time for the very end, witnessing the figure on the podium completely transformed from an hour or so before. There might not have been any blood, but a considerable amount of sweat, blurred with the occasional salty tear, exuded a heady cocktail of physical and emotional exhaustion, and made me realise that although I'd missed the journey, all those involved in it had travelled a significantly long way. As a seven- or eight-year-old, I was far too young to articulate any more than that, but the need for orchestral music to be coaxed and controlled, driven and steered, is one of the reasons it is a good idea to have one individual in charge. Musicians are perfectly capable of doing these things on their own, of course, but with large groups it is almost impossible to reach a unanimous opinion about the detailed route the music should take. A conductor's responsibility is to create such unanimity – to make sure that every player is able to be part of the same performance.

Music implies togetherness. We talk about making a 'concerted' approach to a situation, or doing something 'in concert' with others. Yet, given the innumerable possibilities of meaning that lie behind a symphony, a movement, even a musical phrase, finding consensus within such a context isn't easy. Composers define the sound, to a certain extent, but it's not their role to restrict the imagination of those who play or hear it. Quite the opposite in fact. Every melody sings, every rhythm dances, every structure tells a story – but precisely what those songs, dances, and stories *are* is up to the performers. Music has to sound together, but it has to be *emotionally* co-ordinated as well. I think it is impossible to achieve one without the other. Performances require unity of expression as well as of execution. Music should feel free, but it also has to sound intentional. Especially classical music. Every note is a consequence of the one that precedes it, and is given meaning by the one that comes next. There is an intention behind every sound, an intention that – in an overarching orchestral sense – is led by the conductor.

Schopenhauer wrote about music being simple to understand yet impossible to explain. But although the abstract nature of music enables it to speak to so many, its lack of definability can create a problem when performers need to agree on what a piece means. An orchestra can have as many different opinions as there are players within it, and while none of those views is necessarily wrong, if every opinion is expressed simultaneously, the power of the music will be so diluted that the audience's experience is compromised.

This potential loss of specificity is one of the reasons some people prefer chamber music. They value the intensity of a connection with the composer made the more direct by being created by fewer intermediaries. The sheer mass of an orchestra can work against the music unless its power is concentrated into as defined a conduit as possible. But orchestral music need be neither diffuse, nor emotionally detached. It is profound, wide-ranging, and subtle, and conductors encourage the musicians to relish wearing their hearts on their sleeves while imperceptibly massaging this expression into a focused and sincere line of communication, one that is strengthened, rather than weakened, by the number of people taking part.

When Debussy related music to infinity, he was doing so in a mathematical context – there is a limitless number of ways notes can be combined. But there is an infinite range to their expressive qualities as well. Music might not be able to describe a teaspoon, yet in one phrase it can portray heart-aching joy or invite deep sorrows of sadness with just a single chord. Even so, no amount of metaphorical language can do justice to the precise meaning that we take from hearing it, especially as that meaning is likely to be slightly different for each one of us.

The equivocal nature of music arises to some extent from the limitations of its notation. However, as with the international language Esperanto, its simplicity is predicated on there being a very wide margin for what each sign or symbol means. Music is about a lot more than playing the right notes, or even, as Eric Morecambe disputed, doing so in the right order. In reality no composer's instructions can be anything other than ambiguous. Even highly sophisticated and detailed notation is a relatively rudimentary means of imparting information. There are as many different ways of colouring an individual note as there are of expressing the exactness or flexibility of a particular rhythm. You cannot say a word without meaning. Nor play a sound without interpretation. Even an avoidance of expression is a form of expression in itself. And although a composer might try to define a note's rhythm, volume, accent, length, colour, and speed, these are all essentially subjective attributes and unquestionably all affected by their context. Fortunately, it is the limitations of musical notation that permit limitless possibilities as to its meaning. The finite creates the infinite. And it is the infinite that allows classical music to live on and on. If every performance of Rachmaninov's Second Piano Concerto sounded exactly the same, few would want to hear it again and again and again and again.

Even if all the qualities of an individual note could be defined exactly, it is only in relation to others that it has meaning. Music is about the relationship between the notes, not the notes themselves. It is in this in-between space that expression lies. Between the notes. Between the beats. It is in how you space them apart, how you glue them together, how you connect their consequences or contradict the expectations they create that you metamorphose the printed music into its multi-dimensional expression.

If you listen to a computerised sample of a piece of music, you realise what a difference the player makes. Sometimes even the most famous works can be hard to recognise when divorced from the individual colour of the instruments they were intended for, or the humanity of the musicians who perform them. It is the *imperfections* that define the character of our music-making, and our thought-provoking fallibility is one of the main reasons why machines are yet to replace us altogether.

The impression that a piece is limited rather than set free by the composer's instructions is understandable, given that most people's first exposure to classical music as a child is based on the importance of playing exactly what is written. The idea that the score is the end rather than the means is easily perpetuated by those who might feel threatened by the concept of music being a medium of self-expression. On the other hand, the emphasis that jazz places on improvisation encourages a greater sense of ownership from the player, a connection that is engaging to listen to, not only because the audience can recognise that the music-making is truly personal to the performer, but also that this guarantees the uniqueness of what they are hearing. The relationships that jazz and classical musicians have with their composers are different but, philosophically speaking, I don't think they need be as antithetical as they are perceived as being. The opportunity to integrate yourself with a classical piece of music is less obvious than it is with jazz but it is still crucial if the performance is to sound sincere and significant. Music cannot be a free-for-all. And I am sure most jazz musicians would agree. It is just that they are very good at disguising the rules and principles that underpin the choices they make.

Considering the choices available in classical music, it is possible to justify many different interpretations. But disagreement, inconsistency, or vagueness within a performance is not an option, and most orchestral music-making benefits from a conductor helping to prevent them. The life of a piece of music is like a river. On the surface it always looks the same but underneath there are a myriad elusive configurations that over time subtly alter its overall shape. Its truth is ever changing and musicians have to be open to that instability, embrace it even, while knowing that a performance needs to be consistently true to itself if it is to be successful in conveying meaning.

For conductors to be able to realise their musical ideas, they have to be able to persuade other musicians to accept them. A professional orchestra has a contract to honour the conductor's view but, other than at the most superficial level, a good performance depends partly on the conductor's psychological understanding of those who are actually playing. A talent for inspiring others remains the key component in a conductor's life. However strong our musicianship, it is an irrelevance if we cannot impress it on others.

Yet a skill to convince an orchestra goes only so far. The musicians need to be able to express themselves as well. This is why it is so inappropriate to read about the players performing 'under' a particular conductor. The phrase implies downtrodden musicians, and probably the music too, being 'beaten' into submission. Such a relationship can never result in music-making that reveals more than the limit of one individual's experience. Conductors have to put their personality into the orchestra. But we have no right to own the personalities of the musicians. Our job is to embrace these individual psyches; only by doing so do we get into a position to influence them. Ultimately influence is all we have. It is certainly nothing like the level of control that an audience might imagine. If you really seek command over what you want to express, you are far better off writing a book.

A friend recently told me that her son thought I was extremely clever. He said it was incredible that someone could 'wave a stick up and down all day – and never hit himself in the face'. I am happy to take a compliment from anywhere, especially when it's the unbiased opinion of a six-year-old, but I'd like to think that there's a little more to it than that. Maybe not. Perhaps there's a danger in overthinking things, and I suspect in any walk of life the most successful people don't waste time analysing their challenges or accomplishments. In the end, it is the most natural who are the most believable.

This book is not intended to be an instruction manual for conductors, nor is it a history of conducting. Conducting is not a 'one-size-fits-all' profession. Everybody navigates their own way through the situations they find themselves in, and those who achieve the most are often the ones who are the most individual in their solutions. For, with the best, there is always an unaccountable ingredient. And even if one could unlock that secret, it would have no relevance to one's own character or personality. But, still, I hope that a basic explanation of the musical, physical, and psychological relationship between an orchestra and its conductor, and an exploration of some of the more public and personal issues conductors face, will answer any curiosity audiences might have about the process they are watching, and as a result appreciate even more the music they are hearing.

Music is invisible, and, at its best, leadership is too. Conductors give shape to musical performances, as well as to the practical and psychological processes that precede them. Shaping the invisible might appear either vague or transcendental but beneath the surface a conductor's craft is both specific and deeply human.

1

Conducting Movements

The body never lies.
Martha Graham

In most cases, a conductor's passion for music will have been kindled from an early age. Learning to play an instrument as a child initiates a fundamental relationship with composers that for most musicians offers lifelong reward. The seeds of this relationship are nurtured with hard work and patience, neither of which could be described as run-of-the-mill qualities in an average five-year-old. But technical challenges are best met before the hard-wiring of the teenage nervous system sets in, and endless hours of solitary practice link the formative years of most professional musicians. Such youthful dedication creates a connection that facilitates the camaraderie of the profession, and there is a shared, if unspoken, understanding of the sacrifices that everyone has made while growing up. There is a human bond even before the music turns this into an artistic one.

Conductors choose, perhaps subconsciously, to take one step away from that bond and, in doing so, opt for a more semi-detached professional life. I don't believe the vast majority of conductors think of themselves as better musicians than the players in the orchestra, but there's no denying that the job sets us apart, and the choice we make to move from sitting within a circle of egalitarian music-making to standing at its edge to direct proceedings from the sidelines is a relatively unusual one. The initial decision might have been musical but its consequences affect your life as a whole, and the personal, social, and financial ramifications are just as significant as the musical ones. Even if these are not a valid indication of who you are, they go a long way to affect how you are perceived by everyone else.

There are many different reasons why conductors want to make an entire orchestra the outlet for their love of music. Some might simply not have been good enough on their instrument for it to have been worth them pursuing a career as a performer. Others might have felt that their instrument did not offer enough musical variety, and that the almost limitless repertoire of the symphony orchestra was a more fulfilling vehicle through which to express themselves. There are also those for whom the essentially human dynamic of an orchestra was the most appealing aspect of the job. For me, and I imagine many others, it was a combination of all three. But whatever the motivation, following the career path of a conductor is less a realisation of your skills as a musician than an honest reflection of who you are as a person. In that sense it's not a choice at all. You are who you are and if your personality is more comfortable on its own than in a group, that is a trait that you need to respect. Some people feel more secure as an individual than within a team, and I suspect whether you choose to be a tennis player or a footballer probably says as much about your psyche as it does about your talent.

The idea that the orchestra itself is an instrument on which the conductor plays is a misconception – even if this is an image occasionally fuelled by the reluctance of some in the conducting profession to contradict such delusions of grandeur. But notwithstanding a few material idiosyncrasies and the undoubted personal connection many instrumentalists feel with their unique piece of wood, metal, or brass, the suggestion that a large group of individual musicians is akin to an inanimate object is a significant misunderstanding of the relationship between conductor and orchestra. Although it can sometimes be tempting to wish that the same player would give the same musical response to the same physical gesture on every single occasion, the ever-changing variety of all the people involved is always going to be more interesting than any kind of musical machine.

Conductors do not 'play the orchestra' any more than theatre directors 'play the actors'. It's true that we have a direct involvement in the performance, but we still don't make any of the sounds ourselves. If we have a relationship with any instrument at all, it would perhaps be a fairer analogy to say that it is with our own physicality. This is how we express ourselves. This is how we shape the invisible, and as such, it is through our own body that we need to learn to 'speak'. Although verbal communication is tolerated in rehearsals, it is never especially welcomed in performance. At the most important part of the musical process, a conductor's expression has to be visual not verbal.

In 1971, a study by Albert Mehrabian concluded that face-to-face communication, specifically of feelings and attitudes, could be broken down into three separate components: the words we use (7 per cent), the tone of voice with which we use them (38 per cent), and our body language while we do so (55 per cent). And if the words themselves are contradicted by the speaker's non-verbal behaviour, the latter is the more likely to be believed. Although the results of this research are often oversimplified, it's clear that some form of physiological expression lies at the heart of human communication. Without it the role of the conductor would be very different. Physicalising emotion is something people do every day. Conductors simply take a basic fact of life and use it as a means of creating a clarity of musical style and a strength of emotional feeling.

There are distinct advantages to expressing your attitude to the music with your body alone. However specific the emotion is, it is stronger if not limited by a choice of vocabulary. Words can be easily misunderstood. We all have our own set of linguistic references, and the players' reaction to what they hear us say is unlikely to be as unanimous as their response to what they see us show. Music turns the complicated into the simple but using words to discuss it can easily do the reverse. It is a universal language, yet one that cannot be translated. Body language is the only other means of communication that comes as close to describing the indescribable. Conducting is a combination of the two.

*

One of the things that distinguishes music from speech is its propensity for regular rhythm. We talk in phrases that often lilt towards a form of melodic inflection. But although every sentence has a rhythm of its own, only in exceptional cases does this rhythm lead to an expectation of its pattern being repeated. Human beings are very good at keeping time and our reliable grasp of rhythmic gesture and pulse is why so many mnemonics have a rhythmic basis to them. We often use rhythm to embed things deeply into our brain. And because our brain responds so significantly to rhythm, it's the rhythm of a piece that turns the listener into an active participant. Even if we are not specifically marching or dancing, rhythm activates the brain far more than melody or harmony. It is rhythm that has the power to move people the most – sometimes physically as well as emotionally – and like a poet's use of prosody, a subtle manipulation of the listener's rhythmic expectation is a simple yet profound tool for expression.

Rhythm is the quality of the music's movement and how strict or loose rhythms should sound is a matter of expressive opinion. A composer specifies the music's notes and rhythms, yet neither is an exact science. A pitch can be inflected up or down for an expressive end with the vast majority of instruments and most humans can detect at least ten different frequencies within any one note. But control of rhythm is an even more fundamental part of every performer's contribution to the interpretation of the piece, and the level of rhythmic freedom, insistence, stasis, or rigour is a valuable means of musical storytelling. Our attitude to expressive movement reveals a lot. Even a piece as rhythmically free as Vaughan Williams's *The Lark Ascending* offers performers a choice in how muscular they want the bird to sound. The greater the rhythmic emphasis the less likely the sense of carefree flight. Emotion is energy in motion. And in an orchestra the lead for this emotional energy comes from the conductor. A physically controlled conductor will channel the music's energy with a clarity that players find easy to understand. A good technique can unambiguously express an untold range of pulses, whether the music is as static as a moonlit lake or as hectic as a desert storm.

It is difficult for conductors, especially inexperienced ones, to practise expressing rhythmic energy without the reality of the sound, and of those making the sound, in front of them. Hearing an imaginary sound is limited in its relevance, but there is still value in learning how to become comfortable with your own physicality in private before facing the pressures of needing to be comfortable with it in public. Waving your arms about at home is not as stupid as it looks. It becomes comical only if the motivation for doing so is a vain one. Conducting along to a recording is harmless fun for an amateur who has no real desire to stand up in front of an orchestra, but as a means of practice for a conductor it is pointless. Even if you like the interpretation of the recording you are 'conducting', the experience inevitably forces you to follow the sound you hear rather than discover in yourself the physical responsibility for creating it in the first place. You are just dancing in reaction to the music's energy, not actually generating it. A conductor has no practical equivalent of an instrumentalist's scales but the benefit of developing a familiarity with your own movements is not insignificant. A physical dexterity and calmness is something orchestras find very reassuring, and it is equally reassuring for conductors to be able to trust in the muscle habits that frequent gestural repetition creates.

Every conductor's body is different, and every conductor's technique unique. Physical habits and characteristic gestures are related to whether we are tall or short, lean or not, and our natural posture underlies our appearance when we conduct. If our body is indeed our 'instrument', it stands to reason that we should learn to use it well, and good technique for a conductor is essentially the same as it is for any instrumentalist: an awareness and mastery of one's muscle movements in order to produce a desired result. Conductors who have no command of their own bodies have no direct control of an orchestra. They might achieve what they want through other means but if everything has to be explained and rehearsed without, or in spite of, the visual signals a conductor is giving, it will take significantly longer to achieve. The practical and financial implications of that are obvious but the loss of musical freshness and imaginative freedom that comes from excessive description and repetition can be even more damaging.

Great conductors rarely get complimented on their technique alone. Technique is a means to an end, and assuming your body has a natural ease of uninhibited motion, it will be intrinsically linked to the music you are conducting. Physical clarity is meaningless, if not impossible, when divorced from a clear understanding of the music itself, and an unequivocal belief in one's own view of that music is crucial to being able to show it. A confused or broad-brushed musical opinion leads to a vague and indecisive physicality. This in turn produces a similarly generic musical response from the orchestra. But when conductors are convinced as to what the music is saying, this conviction physically communicates itself directly, and unavoidably, to the players. There are a hundred different ways the opening of Beethoven's Fifth Symphony can be played, and a seasoned orchestral player will probably have played most of them. Although it probably would be possible to achieve a unanimous response through understanding the purely physical leadership an orchestra needs, separating a technical solution from a musical one will never be fully persuasive. Lead with the music and the body should follow.

The clarity of our gestures is a direct result of the clarity of thought and feeling that lie behind them, and when our physical motions are a true consequence of the music's emotions, there is no difficulty in them generating the relevant expression in others. I know from personal experience that whenever an orchestra I am conducting is untogether, it is almost always the result of a musical indecision on my part that my body then subconsciously communicates. Nine times out of ten I can tell a microsecond in advance that I will hear the uncertainty of what I just felt. Doubt and disappointment are a combination worth working hard to avoid.

*

The first thing most conductors do when standing in front of an orchestra is to try to establish a physical connection with the players. Every orchestra has its own physicality, and although the players will adapt in order to fit their conductor of the day, it is often easier, and quicker, if we do most of the adjustment ourselves. There is only one of us, after all. Sometimes it can feel as if you are thrashing around in the dark searching for something to hold on to, but I've learned that it is better if you can be open to letting the connection come to you. That is not a passive solution, but an understanding that the orchestra is looking for something to grasp as well. You might feel all at sea but if you give the hysterical impression you are being attacked by a fish, that only makes it more complicated for anyone to come and help. You are not seeking anything specific, but you know it when you find it, and the ensuing sense of synchronicity is comforting and empowering for both conductor and orchestra alike. Without it one has very little control and certainly minimal fulfilment from what can then feel like a purely coincidental relationship. Knowing when to collect and when to release the energy of the players are musical and psychological questions, but it is one's physicality that reveals the answers. It is the physical relationship between orchestra and conductor that defines the quality of the communication between them.

Nietzsche said that we listen to music with our muscles. It would seem logical therefore to believe that in reverse musical choices can be made in response to what we see. I once heard that a very famous conductor began a rehearsal with an equally celebrated orchestra by conducting them in a G major scale. Whether this anecdote is true or not, the seriousness behind the undoubted humour of the situation is that he wanted to establish a physical relationship with the musicians before they started playing any music.

An invisible thread of connection could be spun separate from the specific demands of whichever piece they were about to rehearse.

A link between music and physicality runs deep. It's probably not a coincidence that most works are divided into sections known, in some languages, as 'movements'. Just as young children can distinguish the varied character of different pieces of music and improvise dances accordingly, the ability of performers to convert gestural shape into musical meaning is intuitive. Apparently human beings are unique in being the only animals able to synchronise their movements to music. Contrary to some people's perception of conductors, it appears that in fact a monkey would not be able to do a better job. Good news for the conductor. Bad news for the monkey.

★

It is human nature for an orchestra player to start to form an opinion of the conductor as a person first and as a musician second. The impression we make matters as soon as we enter the rehearsal room. Some take a politician's view that 90 per cent of power is in the perception of power, and that surrounding themselves with the trappings of authority is going to make asserting it easier. They make a grand arrival, maybe even engineer a late one, in order to create a hierarchy that they might not feel qualified to trust on purely musical grounds. But the relative intimacy of the relationship between orchestra and conductor means players see through such disingenuousness instantly. A sprinkling of bravado is no bad thing but sincerity trumps pretentiousness every time. It is the most genuine conductors who have the most authority.

At the other end of the spectrum, a perceived lack of confidence is equally problematic and can be transmitted physically just as much as verbally. In many cases nerves come from a place of respect for the situation, an appreciation of the knowledge and experience of the orchestra, a recognition of the expectation of the audience, and an understanding of the demands of the music itself. How you deal with that awareness privately is one thing; how you reveal it physically is another. An orchestra is not going to feel comfortable if it doesn't think its conductor is comfortable.

There are some conductors whose charm and innate ability to light up a room and be the centre of any stage can achieve a great deal. They make people feel good about themselves. Then there are others who have all but no charisma away from the music. Charisma is not something that can be learned, but for those lucky enough to have it, such presence attracts opportunities, and eases relationships with large groups of people. It was actually only a hundred years ago that the German sociologist and philosopher Max Weber first connected charisma to the idea of leadership through force of personality alone. Its true meaning is religious in origin, denoting a special power to perform miracles, divinely bestowed by the Holy Spirit – enough perhaps to make even the most egocentric of conductors blush.

On the whole people relate well to those who are neither too confident nor too insecure but, given the professional imbalance in authority between conductor and orchestra, in this context matters are not so straightforward. The players expect, and to an extent require, someone larger than life standing up in front of them. Apart from anything else it needs to be clear to them why they didn't make the choice to do the job themselves. Yet any sign that a conductor is pretending will be immediately apparent. It is hard not to be conscious of the need for this balance when you first meet an orchestra and I often feel that once you actually start conducting, you have negotiated the most complex aspect of the physical dynamic between you. For in the end all that really matters to orchestra players is the quality of the musician standing in front of them. Luckily we have more control over that than over more fundamental aspects of our character, and how our own particular blend of confidence and doubt manifests itself to others.

The easiest way to give the impression of being at ease with yourself is to be at ease with yourself. That's more easily said than done if you are about to embark on something difficult. Music is difficult. It is not easy to get everything right without playing safe. It's a challenge to achieve something special. As the person responsible for enabling an orchestra to want to risk that challenge, a conductor has to be the one who lights the spark in the first place. From the moment we first appear in front of the players, our physical demeanour can relax and inspire them in equal measure. Or not. But a humility about the recreative and collaborative role we are about to undertake with the musicians, as well as a self-confidence that shows we have an unshakeable belief in our right to stand on the podium and conduct them, is not a bad place to start.

★

It is hard to say whether the origin of the conductor's podium was practical or psychological. I suspect a little of both. Clearly it helps those at the back of a large orchestra to see the conductor's physical gestures but there is probably something emotional going on as well. Some conductors make a point of eschewing a rostrum in an effort to avoid it being viewed as a personal pedestal. Others do away with it simply because they are very tall. But the sense of formality and structure that it gives can be valuable in separating the professional relationship from the personal one. The podium can be a way of a conductor saying, 'I am in charge at the moment because I am standing on this box, but when I get off it my opinions, musical or otherwise, are no more valid than anyone else's.' It is a professional convention that reflects the formality of the preparation process. In the broadest of terms, the conductor is in charge – of the music, and of the rehearsal itself – and the podium is a confirmation of that status. It need not necessarily imply the desire to feed a Napoleonic power complex.

Elevated or not, the conductor always needs to be seen by the players. Having to read the music directly in front of them means that that is their primary focus, but peripheral vision is an impressive thing. It might not look as if musicians are watching, but it is relatively hard for them to ignore the only person in the room who is standing up and moving about, and whose physical energy is directly aimed at encouraging something from them.

Players want both practical confidence and imaginative freedom from a conductor's physical stance. Ideally you appear both grounded and flexible – like a tree whose deep roots support balance and energy, whose steadfast trunk suggests wisdom and strength, with supple branches that resist or reveal the winds of change, and whose leaves are constantly shifting shapes and shades, dancing with the light of the air and the rhythm of the spirit. Your body needs to move in both poetry and prose, and to reflect a grammar of musical language that allows endless adjectives and adverbs to colour the structure they are supporting. There needs to be a physical grasp of time that makes it clear whether the music is travelling or arriving, striving uphill, or rolling down. I believe you can show whether the music is of the night or the day, inside or out, private or public. You can make it sound like a vivid oil painting or an impressionistic watercolour, or draw its lines like a refined etching or a rougher woodcut. I'm not sure if you can make it smell like honeysuckle or taste like an onion but the more multi-sensory you are able to be, the more powerfully will your imagination be transmitted to the orchestra.

It does not surprise me that there are people with chromesthesia – the condition that evokes colours when listening to music. It is quite common for people to talk about the range of colours musicians elicit from their instruments, and composers often choose their keys on the basis of which one suggests the emotional colour they want the music to express. We can tell from his operas that Mozart felt that A was most suitable for romantic love. Beethoven wrote much of his heroic music in E flat. C often seems to be favoured for its magisterial associations. As it is possible to express a certain emotion physically, one can by extension conduct a certain tonality. It is an esoteric idea, but I have played games with students in which the group has to guess the key the young conductor is expressing. The success rate is gratifyingly high.

We cannot conduct the meaning of an individual note. But we can affect the meaning of the relationship that two notes have with one another. We can show whether the music is angry or sad, desperate or hopeful, private or communal, pink or blue. And we should. Our job is to help turn the music's black and white dots into a rainbow of light and shade, releasing its lines into a host of different contours and colours. The limitations of musical notation demand a metaphorical translation of what is written in the orchestra musician's part. And the fantasy of each individual player's imagination needs to be channelled towards a unified orchestral opinion.

*

In a metaphysical sense the core of a creative musical experience hovers somewhere in the middle of a triangle formed by composer, conductor, and orchestra. In some mysterious way, everyone travels towards this musical centroid and it is by making this journey that the uniqueness of any performance is created. If everyone is open to the idea of being influenced by something they had not thought of before, the potential for musical discovery is rich. Conductors are in a position to instigate that quest, indeed have a responsibility to do so, and it is their arms that are the most conspicuous tools for embracing this role. Conductors who keep their arms too close to their body run the risk of seeming as if they are claiming ownership of the music for themselves. But if their arms are too outstretched they won't be able to suggest a magnetic concentration that can bring a large orchestra together. Ideally, you give the impression that the music and the situation are one, but do so with a sort of virtual hug that somehow releases the sound rather than encloses it.

The strength, mobility, and flexibility of our hands are extraordinary. Their vast range of movement offers limitless opportunities for communication, and we subconsciously associate their nerve-rich tactile nature with a great deal of sensory perception. We need only look at Rodin's sculptures to appreciate how expressive hands can be. And those are not even moving. Dexterity can be a thing of beauty in its own right. Hands seem to speak a primordial language, with a vocabulary that no one who seeks to be understood ignores. Politicians consciously choose to exaggerate their hand gestures to enforce their rhetoric, and in – we hope – a more poetic context, conductors constantly use them to send out a vast range of subliminal messages. Hands can caress and command in equal measure. Fingers can encourage a delicate fragility of sound, or a detailed precision of articulation, while the passion and determination of a clenched fist feels like a gesture from the very beginning of time.

Given our hands' expressive capabilities, it makes complete sense that some conductors choose not to use a baton. Choral conductors almost always use their hands alone, feeling, I imagine, that this better serves the human voice, the pure humanity of which might be compromised by the intrusion of a piece of wood, plastic, or fibreglass. Yet, for as long as people have tried to keep musicians together, many have employed some form of stick – arguably humankind's first ever tool – to do so. In what might be the first recorded instance of a conductor, Pherekydes of Patrae waved a golden staff at his musicians in 709 BC, and had the seventeenth-century French composer–conductor Jean-Baptiste Lully been a little less forceful with his floor-stamping cane, his foot might not have sustained the injury that eventually led to his death from gangrene. The idea that a white stick can create greater rhythmic and emotional precision is debatable. However, with a good technique a baton can be as nimble as any finger, and has the potential to be an unequivocal yet gentle beacon of authority.

Orchestra players vary in where they consider the focal point of a beat to be. Some may instinctively watch the hand; others look to the end of the stick. It is problematic if the conductor offers a contradiction between the two. But if the hand serves the stick and not the other way around, there will be no confusion, and a baton can be a beautiful instrument with which a conductor can lead the music's character as well as its pulse. Moved like a bow, its speed and pressure through the air can generate simultaneous qualities from string players; it can offer a more exact fixed point around which wind players can predetermine their breathing, and those towards the back of the orchestra will benefit from the beat being magnified by the wider trajectory that such an extension can describe. A baton can suggest the longest of musical lines or the smoothest of shapes; it can insist with lightness and grace, or coax with depth and sonority.

Conductors who enjoy using a baton care a great deal about what it feels like. If it is to be a valid extension of our hand it needs to connect to the fingers and palm in exactly the right way. The individual precision and comfort of this requires a careful choice from a wide range of batons and many conductors have their batons made especially for them. Personally I am indebted to a Polish professor of experimental physics at University College London. Conducting with a stick that doesn't feel right is like a violinist using someone else's bow. It is physically possible but a difference in balance and weight severely inhibits an ability to express oneself with confidence. And without confidence you are like a bird without feathers. As Adlai Stevenson said, 'It's hard to lead a cavalry charge if you think you look funny on a horse.'

★

Despite the power of body language, and the importance of a strong stance, open posture, inviting arms, revealing hands, and a clear stick technique, most orchestra musicians will tell you that they actually look at the conductor's face for the most significant signs of communication. The eyes, the 'windows of the soul', tell the most interesting story. They reveal your understanding of the music, your confidence in your own opinions, and your trust in the players. Or they divulge the opposite of those things. They never lie.

Well, almost never. People naturally assume that our facial expression is a sign of what we are thinking. But this is not always the case. Most of us supposedly have a 'resting face', an unintentional expression that shows itself in a certain way when we are particularly engrossed. Conductors are unlucky if their thinking face makes them look as if they are stern or uninvolved, but if that is the case, awareness of it can cause even more problems. To remember to smile every time you are concentrating is almost impossible, and even if you succeed you will probably come across as insincere at best, weird at worst. It works the other way round too. I am always taken aback when a player I have been convinced from their countenance has hated every single minute of the rehearsal expresses exactly the opposite to me when it is over. It's hard not to be affected by what we perceive to be a natural expression of feelings but the potential for misunderstanding is always there.

American psychologist Paul Ekman believes we are capable of around ten thousand different facial expressions. Reassuringly for conductors who work in foreign countries, it seems most facial expressions apply universally across every human culture. These include anger, disgust, fear, joy, sorrow, surprise, amusement, contempt, contentment, embarrassment, excitement, guilt, pride, relief, satisfaction, and shame. That's probably just about enough for a Mahler symphony. Conductors have to be a 'facebook' of musical expression, while at the same time making sure it is the music's emotional story, not our own, that we are reflecting. The most personal of feelings can be rendered sentimental or embarrassing if shared too publicly, and the line between uninhibited and self-indulgent is a fine one, a line that can be sincerely found by conductors whose motivation encompasses an acceptance that the music is not about them. The best conductors appear like a vessel through which the music flows because that is how they see themselves too.

Conductors bare a great deal of their own soul and personality. But the best express a vast range of emotional extremes without actually attaching any of their own essential self to the experience. They create intensity without any tension of their own. They relax up, not down, and generate enormous freedom without losing their own inner control. This allows the players to join the emotional journey of the piece without it involving personal commitment to the conductor. A universal expression of the composer's personality, rather than the conductor's, is inevitably going to speak to more people more deeply. To be able to express without expressing within is a rare gift indeed.

Audiences rarely see the conductor's face, and so seldom witness this fundamental part of the communication. I'm glad that this is the case and am always slightly embarrassed by the presence of listening watchers, or watching listeners, behind the orchestra. I wonder if I have given away any trade secrets – or personal ones for that matter. A conductor's signals are intended for the players, not for the public. They are the palette and the brush, not the painting. Our emotional expression is a visual means to an audible end and it's problematic if the cart is visibly ahead of the horse. But although I don't believe an audience should experience the music through the physicality of the conductor, there is no hiding the fact that we are the most individually visible part of the performance. It is simply not realistic to expect to be ignored, especially as studies have shown that what audiences see does indeed influence what they hear. Evidently a visually high level of passion is considered to be an audible one as well. Whether we like it or not, it seems what we look like does undoubtedly have an impact on the public's perception of the concert.

I used to think that the orchestra musicians were the sole channel through which the music was communicated and my physicality was intended for their benefit alone. But I now realise that it is logical for conductors' gestures to have a direct, albeit probably subconscious, musical effect on the experience of the audience. If I am focusing my attention on the double-bass players at the climax of Beethoven's Seventh Symphony for instance, while the rest of the orchestra is playing the more obvious tune, it stands to reason that anyone in the audience who is watching me will also become more conscious of the significance of this particular part. It's rather similar to the influence camera directors have on a concert filmed for television. Their choice of shots and angles effectively edits the experience for the viewer watching and listening at home.

There is probably no harm in a conductor's arms leading the audience's ears, as long as this is a consequence of our gestures, and not the purpose of them. But people have come to listen to the music, not watch a lecture on it, and you want an audience to hear the sum of the musical parts, rather than its individual wheels and cogs. Still, although the overall structure and emotional intensity of the piece is going to be obvious to people listening with their eyes closed, some of its more subtle details are definitely supported by an audience's visual recognition that they are there. Playing *for* the gallery is not the same thing as playing *to* the gallery, especially if you can avoid being distracted by the damaging self-awareness that acknowledging this can lead to.

Clearly the level of our physical engagement must be appropriate to the energy of the music. It would be distracting to look as if you were taking part in a boxing match if the music was meant to sound like a game of croquet. And you should probably not behave as if you were at a royal garden party if the music sounds as if it's coming from Madison Square Garden. Not that I have been to either. People should be able to tell just by watching whether you are conducting a symphony by Haydn or Shostakovich. But our energy level also has to be a reflection of the needs of the musicians. A complicated and hysterical section of music can be best served by an economy of movement that makes sure there is no extra confusion for the players. Often, the more I beat, the more opportunity for misunderstanding I feel I create. An emotion might be big but extremely passionate gestures can sometimes just offer a greater possibility of disorientation.

Luckily, most of the time the musical and practical energy requirements are one and the same. Except that it is not a matter of luck. In a masterpiece, the physical playing of the music is part of the music itself. The greatest composers never wrote anything impossible to play and it's safe to assume that if something is not working technically, the chances are it is the musical choices that are wrong. If good violinists cannot play the end of Brahms's Fourth Symphony, it is probably because they are being asked to do so at a speed that is too fast for the music. But if there is a contradiction between the music and the playing of it, the players' needs should always take priority over the musical ones. There is no point the conductor expressing emotional turmoil if in doing so it becomes impossible for the orchestra to do the same.

It is also true to say that the more physical effort one puts in, the harder it is to listen properly. The more you conduct, the less you hear. Franz Liszt usefully pointed out that conductors 'are steersmen, not oarsmen'. On the other hand, if we don't put enough into the physicality, it's hard to have any influence on the musicians at all. Ideally the pressure of the connection is comparable to the contact a skier has with snow. Good skiers know when to dig in and when to glide, when to control the curve and when to trust the gradient. There is a constant flexing and bending of the knees that allows a natural give and take between skier and mountainside. Deny it at your peril. Although a wrong choice for a skier can have a more catastrophic physical outcome, the potential to fall is there for the conductor too. And it tends to be the orchestra, like the mountainside, that – publicly at least – emerges unscathed.

Nevertheless, conductors have a responsibility to get the most out of the musicians and there are pieces in which one repeatedly has to ask for more than an individual player might think it possible to give. But there is a difference between stretching the orchestra to its limits and demanding that it tries to exceed them. Players look to us for inspiration to push themselves to find that something extra inside them, and they are grateful when they achieve it. But cajoling players to go further than they are capable of, or want to, rarely works. To me at least, a jockey's whip seems to be more a reflection of the rider's personality than the horse's.

★

The origin of the need for a conductor lies in the most basic requirement for musicians to play or sing together, especially in circumstances, musical or otherwise, where it might not be possible for them to hear each other well. Light travels significantly faster than sound, and a visual guide is always going to be more exact than an audible one.

There are patterns for beating time that musicians learn from an early age and grow to relate to subconsciously. Textbooks aplenty explain with arrow-laden illustrations various different ways in which one can navigate this visual geometry in a way that orchestra players find clear. Notwithstanding some opinionated discrepancy on the details of how this musical semaphore is best done, they all agree on one thing: that the first beat of every bar is the most important. It is the most important musically, and it's the one that musicians rely on for confirmation as to where they are in the music. This is especially relevant for those in the orchestra who are counting bars' rest rather than actually playing. It is the silent musicians who need a conductor's architectural clarity the most. Counting a hundred bars' rest can be harder than it sounds if the music is new to the players, and they need, or at least appreciate, a very obvious and consistent physical gesture to be a trustworthy guide. But, although the down-beat is of paramount importance to the silent players, to those who are playing it is the up-beat preceding every down-beat that is far more crucial.

There is a cartoon that shows a conductor whose music stand reveals the instruction: 'Wave your arms around till the music stops, then turn around and bow.' It's amusingly deprecating, but it doesn't explain how the music started in the first place. That's the hard bit. The initial up-beat of a piece, in rehearsal or performance, is the most specific task conductors have. You are aiming to create something out of nothing. It is almost the only time you move in silence. It is the only time you do something that does not accompany the musicians. And it is the only time you are truly alone. From then on everything can be more collaborative and musically consequential. To be honest, I often find it quite a relief to have started.

The very beginning of a piece, or of any movement for that matter, is the only moment you know for sure that every orchestra musician is watching you. And probably everyone in the audience too. You are unquestionably the centre of attention. Establishing with a single motion the music's breath, pulse, sound, volume, mood, temperature, and style needs a concentration of physical energy and a calmness of mind. But apart from the musical and practical need for the up-beat to be clear, the opening gesture also needs to send a message of complete confidence to the musicians, some of whom might quite understandably be feeling nerves of their own. The goal is to be able to dictate with both conviction and trust. Adrenalin and oxytocin in perfect equilibrium.

For me, it helps to imagine that in some sense the music has already started. Your inner ear then provides you with a silent pulse and you can already picture an invisible scene. It means you are somehow joining something that already exists, albeit only to yourself, rather than feeling any pressure to set it in motion in the first place. I don't think there is any shame in privately singing to yourself the violins' opening melody of Mozart's Symphony No. 40 in order to guarantee that you conduct the violas' brief introduction to it at exactly the right speed. You are then showing the confirmation of what you want to achieve, not its initialisation.

Once you have started, every beat is an up-beat to the one that follows it. Except for the very last beat of the piece, each beat is an invitation to the next. And in that invitation lies all the information you aim to impart, the most important of which is creating a certainty about when the conclusion of the beat, and therefore the start of the next invitation, will arrive. The words 'up' and 'down' indicate the direction in which conductors move their arms but they also indicate what the beats should feel like. 'Upbeat' is optimistic. It is an encouraging word. It's good to feel up. 'Downbeat' on the other hand is negative and depressed, even perhaps a little abused. But if every down-beat can be viewed as an up-beat to the next, it is possible to generate a constant feeling of anticipation and lightness, as well as momentum, buoyancy, and flow. And it's no bad thing always to have to have your mind one beat ahead of the music. Consciousness of the future allows you better to take care of the present.

The human brain has a sophisticated ability to judge the relationship between space and time. If a conductor's gestures travel through the air with a clear sense of direction and an inevitable point of arrival, the players feel relaxed enough to be able to prepare their own technique to deliver exactly the right sound at precisely the right moment. An unambiguous beat speed, coupled with a visual certainty as to where the beat will arrive, is the basis of conducting technique. This clarity is what gives the orchestra players confidence in their own sense of pulse and helps them agree on precisely whatever rhythmic freedom and flexibility the music needs. Because their own choice of when and how to play has to be taken in advance, they make those decisions during the up-beat. And the physical preparation they require for the note they are going to play has to be acknowledged by the conductor's gestures. By the time the beat arrives the player is already committed, and if it is a contradiction of what the player has been led to expect, the uncertainty will be audible to everyone. Both the musicians and the music need to breathe, and a sensitivity to the physical and musical dimensions of this breath is the most important skill conductors should have.

★

The point of the bar line is to show the fundamental pulse of the music. In principle, all music pertains to one beat per bar. Yet, in all but the fastest music, bars are divided into more frequent stresses. The composer instructs the performers how many beats each bar should have, but although these inner pulses are prescribed, they are not necessarily what the conductor chooses to beat. The music may have a sense of two beats to every bar, but you might feel that showing only the first of these beats would better prevent the pulse from being overly laboured. Conversely, you might feel that two beats in the bar, particularly in slower music, would be more clearly expressed by subdividing those two beats into four, thereby having greater control over how the two main beats look and therefore sound.

Classical music is rarely that simplistic or consistent, and in reality we have to be open to constantly changing the specific divisions of any particular bar. It is possible to conduct in one, subdivide into two, then go back into one before subdividing again, this time into four. If you can do it well, neither you nor the players will be confused. They will not even notice an inconsistency if your choices mirror the flexibility of the music itself. An underlying pulse can remain unchanged despite the impulses you give it being ever varied.

On this, as on many issues, players have different opinions. Some prefer fewer and therefore slower frequencies of beating and, assuming the conductor is physically reliable, they respond positively to being trusted to work within such a framework. Others are comfortable relating to more

frequent confirmations of the rhythm. A positive relationship with a conductor is often based on a similar approach
as to which is the most appropriate choice to make, but the
range of views on this matter, even within an orchestra, can
be difficult to reconcile.

The decisions conductors make about beating patterns
are related to their view of what the music needs and what
they think the players need, but they are also a reflection
of what they feel most comfortable with themselves. If you
are not happy with your own physical choice, that awkwardness will inevitably transmit itself to the orchestra.
Knowing your own strengths and weaknesses is similar to
an instrumentalist knowing which fingering can be trusted
the most. But it's often more difficult for a conductor than
for an instrumentalist to decide in advance what's going
to work best. The physical reality of sound and the wide
variety of orchestral preferences can produce surprises that
you have to be able to adapt to. It is better not to be too
rigid about predetermining what you do. There have been
several occasions on which I have rethought the best way of
indicating something in response to how an orchestra has
interpreted what I did. Rehearsals are for conductors too.

The vast majority of musical bars can be subdivided into
two or three beats, and by further extension therefore into
four and six. Some beating patterns are more musical to
conduct than others. Personally, I'm more comfortable
with sideways gestures than up-and-down ones. I feel the
binary nature of two-in-a-bar offers limited opportunities
for expression. There's simply not much room to work
with. But lateral movements left and right force you to re-

veal a more personal space. The communication is more open-hearted. Perhaps there's a reason that music in three beats to the bar feels more human to conduct than that in two: would we not rather waltz than march?

More irregular bars, such as those containing five or seven beats, offer a different challenge. Prime numbers cannot be equally divided and the inner imbalance that this creates is often exactly why composers choose them when they want to express some kind of restless ambiguity. It is a shame that we rarely teach these bar lengths to children. Whether it's because we think they are overcomplicated mathematically or because the uncertain emotions they imply are deemed unsuitable for the impressionable, I don't know. But, whatever the reason, we grow up associating music in five or seven with something adventurous, an emotional danger that at some point in the past we might not have been considered ready for by others. I doubt I am the only conductor who feels out of my comfort zone whenever I am called on to be so emotionally irregular yet rhythmically constant.

When it comes to beating time, the most important thing is to make the beginning of every bar visibly unequivocal without the musical line sounding, self-consciously, constantly, interrupted, by annoying, fastidious, punctuation. The grammatical structure of a musical sentence should be as unobtrusive as it is in any other language. There is plenty of music, especially well-known music, in which players do not need to see the down-beat all the time and it can be liberating to feel free from the functional inner workings of the pulse. No one wants to hear musicians' organisational tools any more than they want to look at the Sydney Opera House and see the mechanics that keep it from falling down. The bar line is a necessary evil; its tyranny a common frustration. Like Victorian children, down-beats are expected to be seen but not heard.

★

The original meaning of the word 'symphony' is simply a 'unison of sounds'. Instrumentalists need to be able to play together for music to work. But as important as good ensemble obviously is, it is a means to an end rather than a goal in itself. Extreme pinpointing of the beats can come at an expressive cost. Although conductors have a practical responsibility to show a vertical clarity of moment, we have a musical responsibility to encourage a horizontal sense of lyricism as well. Music is a horizontal art form. It exists only in relation to a real-life timeline. For some reason timelines mean more to us when they are horizontal rather than vertical, and leading and maintaining an imaginary musical line that can fluctuate in parallel to a real one is much easier to do with lateral movements.

There is a theory that suggests that the right hand is for beating time and the left hand is for expression, or the other way around for left-handed conductors. But it's not only simplistic to separate the practical from the expressive; it is impossible. You cannot shape a musical phrase without suggesting its sense of rhythmic movement as well. Nor can you beat time devoid of meaning altogether. A military bandmaster's absence of sentiment can be deeply moving.

However, there is no point in both arms doing the same thing. Players do not need information replicated in mirror image. Given the near impossibility of perfect synchronicity between the two anyway, it is more likely that the arms would simply contradict each other. You should be able to conduct one-handed, and if your arms do not have autonomy of movement, it might be a lot clearer if you did. Richard Strauss thought you should keep your left hand in your waistcoat pocket. But if each arm can give independent yet complementary messages, you are obviously doubling your communication tools. A complicated score could potentially have twenty different things going on at once. Two arms are going to be twice as good as one in trying to enable a clarity of ensemble and create a unity of vision.

Whichever hand it is though, when it comes to the more emotional – as opposed to practical – signals, there is no textbook. There does not need to be. A conductor paints emotion in the air in exactly the same way as someone who is not a conductor would do it. You do not have to be a mime artist to express a wide range of things through gesture alone. An elemental form of human communication, learned from birth, is instinctively expressed and instinctively understood. In that sense alone, conducting is simply child's play.

Conductors show what they believe to be the most important musical voice at any given time, and crudely speaking look at where that voice comes from to share the decision with the orchestra. The musical hierarchy is established mainly by visual contact. But looking at a player is also an opportunity to give them the emotional confidence that they are in the right place. Depending on how well known the piece is, players who might have had to count for a long time before starting to play an exposed or difficult passage will find it considerably easier to do if they have received affirmation and encouragement at the right moment. Given that a cymbal player has only one note in the whole of Bruckner's Seventh Symphony, it would seem inconsiderate not to show that you are conscious of its musical significance. But although it might look like an important part of a conductor's job, bringing in musicians with a visual cue is not strictly necessary. Players have the music in front of them. It tells them what to play and when, and they don't need specific help with what they already know. But the benefits of a conductor sharing the responsibility for musical entrances with the instrumentalists are significant on a human as well as a musical level. Our relationship with the musicians should be equal to our relationship with the music.

*

Ultimately the analogy that the conductor's instrument is our own physicality breaks down because our silent ability to express our own musicianship relies on other people's interpretation of what we are showing, not to say their opinion on whether we are worth responding to at all. And these people, those who actually make the music, are endlessly varied.

There are as many different responses to our physicality as there are musicians and orchestras. It is not a reliable science – thank goodness. Some orchestras play very much with the beat. Others play a little behind it, in part to evaluate whether they agree with you or not, but mainly because the sort of sound they want to make requires time to make it. It can be unnerving to hear such a delayed response, but once you abandon your vanity (no bad thing to do anyway) the only issue is how it sounds. If the music is together and has a quality that you hoped to hear, then there is nothing wrong with the connection feeling like an old-fashioned transatlantic phone call. Once you get used to it, you realise that the sound delay is your problem alone. How you respond to that problem is what matters.

Experience or talent, or both, enables you to engage with whatever you hear in the right way. Waiting for the sound can be a disaster. Not waiting for it can be just as much of a disaster. It is important to know when to adjust to the sound and when to ignore it. No two orchestras are the same, every hall is different, and you have to be able to react to the variety of responses and acoustics you encounter. I don't think you'd get very far, musically or professionally, if you simply saw your role as laying down a law for people to obey. Even if you did have a technique that could perfectly dictate every nuance, every rhythm, and every transition, this would then just ensure that the players' role was simply subservient. At best, this would be a deeply unfortunate missed opportunity.

An ability to adapt physically to what you hear, without losing your responsibility for leadership, is essential. This is the 'leading with' that defines conducting. So when the engineers at SONY built a robot to conduct the first movement of Beethoven's Fifth Symphony, they missed the whole point of what a conductor does. Of course orchestra musicians can follow a robot, but if the robot is not listening to the way in which they are following, there is no room for their own contribution. It forces the players to be robots too. There is a reason 'robotic' can be an insult. Music is one of the things that defines us as human beings and the humanity of music is its greatest strength. Take that away and we are all in trouble. When orchestra players realise that the conductor is listening and responding to what they do, they feel both validated as people and empowered as musicians to be part of the process of the performance.

Conductors have to listen to how the musicians respond to their beat in order to know how to conduct the next beat. There is no contradiction between listening and leading. It is a constant cycle of action and reaction, a virtuous circle of coordinated response that connects the reality of the sound with the sound of your imagination. You have to listen, then hear, then react, then create, and do all these things as instantaneously as possible. Though you instigate the invitation to play, the orchestra's interpretation of that invitation needs to be something that you then agree with – assuming of course that you do. It becomes a shared physicality in which the culmination of your beat coincides with where you hear, and also where you see, the musicians have decided that it is. A conductor takes the lead, engages in how that lead is interpreted, and effectively then joins in. The process is rather a dance. When it is right, this shared physicality is remarkable.

To encourage listening is the main physical objective of a conductor. At its heart music-making is music sharing and the musicians will be the best musicians they can be if their own musical decisions are related to what they hear around them. But it isn't easy to listen and play at the same time. Multitasking is especially hard when the jobs are so contradictory. Playing an instrument demands great personal concentration, but music asks you simultaneously to focus on what other people are doing as well. Conductors have to show that they are listening. Our attention leads the orchestra's attention. And if the players can see that we are making choices as a result of what we hear, they will realise that they can afford to do the same.

If a listening dynamic is well established, the responsibility for the ensemble is no longer visual and therefore hierarchical, but aural and therefore far more collaborative. Even if an orchestra starts to lose its ensemble, sometimes the quickest way for it to recover is for the conductor to all but stop conducting. If you can't beat it, join it. This is not abdicating responsibility, but encouraging a greater sharing of it, acknowledging that the players' ears and their natural musicianship can be a better guide to them finding their way back together than their eyes trained on our – at these moments most likely rather stressed – physicality. Intentionally backing off from physical leadership forces the musicians to listen to each other and, assuming they know that something is wrong, which is not a given considering that it is probably their inability to hear another part of the orchestra that has led to the problem in the first place, encouraging them to take a DIY approach is often the easiest route to a successful solution.

Another advantage of stepping back from time to time, other than it revealing how much you trust the musicians, is that varying the levels of engagement prevents the physical connection between you becoming boring and predictable. There is no point surprising the musicians for the sake of it, but when you want to convey something that you consider to be especially important, this will be more effective if you are not in the habit of insisting on the importance of every single beat.

The best time not to wave one's arms about is when the music itself transcends anything one could possibly want to add to it. There are some moments in some pieces by some composers that are so mysteriously wonderful, so spiritually untouchable, that physicalising them reduces their magic. Enabling the musicians, and the audience as well, to find that most private core of imagination is best achieved by remaining completely still. I think the breathtaking sense of universal stasis at the start of the 'Nimrod' movement in Elgar's *Enigma Variations* is rendered most powerful if the conductor makes almost no physical, and therefore no personal, contribution to it whatsoever. I would not say that not moving is doing nothing. There is still a flow within your stillness. You are always in some sense conducting. But you are doing so in the subtlest of ways. We spend a lot of time coaxing people to let their emotions out, but encouraging people to travel more inwardly, and allowing the music to foster an invisible coming together of everyone in the room, is one of the greatest privileges of conducting. It is a communion of private emotion. Still falls the sound.

The physicality of conducting is not the be all and end all of the job. Paradoxically, what you look like when you conduct need not matter at all. There are plenty of great conductors who achieve miraculous results despite a certain awkwardness or perhaps age-induced frailty. In these instances, good performances spring from a relationship with the orchestra that relies on a personal and musical connection, and as long as that relationship exists in one form or another, players can normally disregard practical problems that may arise from any compromised physicality. In the end it is the orchestra, not the conductor, that plays the music. It is the musicians the audience hears.

2

Conducting Musicians

Without contraries is no progression.
William Blake

A retired boxer once told me that he always got goose-bumps when conductors stepped onto the stage. He said he was in awe of their power. I found his opinion, coming from such a physically intimidating man, ironic to say the least. There are certainly some who wield considerable influence within the profession, but this applies mostly in extra-musical contexts. When it comes to an actual rehearsal or performance, power is anathema to the essential spirit of music-making.

There have been many times, especially when I was less experienced, that I felt distinctly un-powerful. An orchestra is quite capable of ignoring a conductor, and will readily do so if it thinks the audience would benefit as a result. Indeed, some players might even feel a responsibility to disregard the conductor if they believe this would protect the musical experience for the public. Everybody makes mistakes, and professional orchestras can't afford to follow every single gesture made by every single conductor. Although there are times when I've been frustrated by an orchestra not agreeing with my musical opinions, there have been many occasions in which their expertise has saved me from making a hash of something. In an ideal world you want an orchestra to stick to you like a glove, but only up until the moment you make a mistake.

A willingness on the part of the players to resolve problems themselves is related not so much to any power your position as conductor might afford, but rather to how much authority you have been able to exude through musical, physical, or personal means. Power is granted to an individual by others, but authority is a natural ability, the possessor of which, to labour the etymological point, is literally the author. This quality of individual ownership is one of the reasons great conductors differ so much in how they go about their work. Their authority is unique to who they are.

Power often works through fear and can force people to act against their will, through status or physical strength. But authority functions through respect and persuades others to respond voluntarily, simply through personal influence. If conductors ever have to ask musicians to watch or listen to them, it is normally too late to have any effect. The cliché of tapping the stand with the baton in order to attract the attention of the players has long since become outdated, and an orchestra will never deeply engage with you purely because of a conventional hierarchy that some might assume exists. In as creative and human a field as music, it is authority – not power – that is more successful in creating a genuine performance of quality. In the long run, even if it looks less impressive, control without oppression accomplishes far more. Power damages relationships, and its trappings rarely last for ever, but a natural authority, one that stops short of being authoritarian, empowers others and lasts a lifetime. Those blessed with it stay in charge for longer than those whose leadership is circumstantial.

In a musical context, it is noticeable that the same authority doesn't always flourish equally well in every situation. There are many conductors to whom some orchestras respond positively while others do not. Even from day to day, the strength of any one connection can fluctuate. Musicians are emotional people. They have to be. It's not surprising that the mood of a large group of them can be unwittingly and swiftly altered from a positive to a negative. Human nature makes the opposite journey harder to achieve.

Two and a half thousand years ago, the Greek philosopher Xenophon wrote that a leader should be 'ingenious, energetic, full of stamina, and presence of mind. Loving and tough, straightforward and crafty, ready to gamble everything and wishing to have everything. Generous and greedy, trusting and suspicious.' The United States Marines require a more modern set of credentials: justice, judgement, dependability, integrity, decisiveness, tact, initiative, endurance, bearing, unselfishness, courage, knowledge, loyalty, and enthusiasm. It is fascinating how similar these two lists are, despite the centuries that separate them. Human nature doesn't change that much. Nevertheless, I suspect only a few of these character traits are taught at conducting schools. Whether that is because they are considered a result of nature rather than nurture I don't know, but most are personal qualities likely to have been established long . before anyone decides they want to be a conductor.

Henry Ford said that asking who ought to be in charge is like asking who ought to be the tenor in the quartet. Obviously the man who can sing tenor. He suggests that leadership is a collection of attributes that either you have or you don't have. Some conductors possess these attributes in such abundance that orchestras are only too happy to follow, however much they might disagree with the musical opinion on offer. Then there are others who have such an infectious natural musicianship that an absence of leadership skills can often go unnoticed. Clearly a combination of the two would be an orchestra's dream ticket.

In modern society we don't necessarily think of leadership as something that is the province of just one individual. We often hear sports coaches speaking of how they want everyone in their team to be a leader on the pitch. 'Leadership density' is the latest fad phrase. For a conductor this contemporary view of teamwork has both pros and cons. On the one hand creating the unity of interpretation that music demands is extremely challenging within an environment in which everybody feels entitled to a view. But, on the other, enriching that interpretation with the knowledge, experience, and imagination of everyone in the room is always going to lead to more interesting performances.

The legendary stories of severe and ruthless maestros are pretty much a thing of the past. In the old days, a conductor could get away with shouting and screaming at the musicians. Players could be fired on the spot, or sent home after a performance, humiliated, with their concert tails between their legs. It's hard to accept that a climate of fear and intimidation was best suited to delicately phrasing a soft *cantabile* melody. Yet listening to an old recording of Verdi's *Requiem* made by one of the more infamous tyrants is to hear playing of astounding beauty, subtlety, and pathos. It's a mysterious 'success' that is unlikely now. We live at a time when respect for authority is no longer a given. In orchestral terms some believe this has triggered a loss of both distinction and distinctiveness. But music-making led with a breath of civility creates a variety that is more stimulating, and a quality far more profound.

Yet classical music is not completely in tune with the zeitgeist of the day. Contemporary society encourages everybody to be equally individual and collaboration has itself become less celebrated. Orchestral music, however, is nothing without teamwork and leading it demands an ability to inspire such an approach. Like most people in leadership positions, conductors get their perceived power from making other people powerful. In music, even if you can force someone to play a phrase in a way they don't agree with, it will never sound that convincing. Orchestras prefer to be stirred, not shaken. Musical leadership – all leadership – is more about enlightening than dominating.

Some musicians want their conductors to be approachable; others want to be able to keep their distance. There are probably just as many who want us to be 'everyman' as there are who seek something more unusual. Knowing how different individuals need to be led is probably a key to succeeding as a leader in the first place. But it can be dangerous to overthink things. Being yourself is more important than being who you think some people might want you to be. Even though you might have to highlight some aspects of your character more than others, you are who you are. Better to adjust the volume than twiddle the dial in search of another channel. Therein lies only madness.

The best symphonic experiences occur when each member of the orchestra feels empowered to take ownership of the performance. Such collective responsibility can be instigated by conductors who have the confidence that players will respond to their trust, and when players can trust themselves and their fellow musicians to respond, the music-making can be both free and purposeful – like a flock of starlings patterning the sky with effortless conviction and seemingly invisible leadership.

The best analogy I know for conducting is the image of trying to keep a songbird in your hand. Grasp it too tightly and you will crush it; hold it too loosely and it will fly away. Overbearing leadership suffocates musicians, but offer no leadership whatsoever and the result will be disparate. It's a question of balance, and where one positions the fulcrum varies depending on how much the musicians want to be controlled or trusted. Not every player responds well to a laissez-faire approach. Conductors need either an instinctive gift or extremely well-focused intuition to know when and whom to trust, and when and whom to push. This applies to the piece as well. Impose too much of ourselves on the music and we'll stifle the composer; not enough and the performance will be bland. As every piece is different, rehearsals are partly about coming to an agreement about when the music has to be exactly in time and when it needs space to breathe. I suspect the best way to create unity as well as freedom is not to see the two as opposites in the first place. Discipline need not be tyrannical and accuracy does not have to imply rigidity. Nor does a lack of either always lead to chaos. Flexibility is not the same thing as compromise.

The most important thing about control, whether of yourself or others, is that it has no purpose in and of itself. If the motivation is right, control doesn't feel like controlling, and if it is something you use rather than something you rely on, players understand that it is a necessary and valuable part of the job. But orchestra musicians love to be allowed simply to play, and, assuming they embrace the responsibility that that trust requires in return, this is what most conductors want too. It's much simpler for one person to accept the ideas of the group than the other way around. Experience tells you when to accept the things you cannot change or change the things you cannot accept.

A young, insecure, or inexperienced conductor might imagine that sharing the reins could be seen as a sign of weakness or indecision. But being open to other ideas doesn't imply being devoid of them yourself. It boils down to trust: a mutual trust in which the conductor appreciates that players can express themselves as individuals without becoming anarchists, and orchestra musicians know in return that they can take on board a conductor's vision without necessarily having to sacrifice their own. The best musicians see no contradiction between the ego and the team. It's the same in any form of group creativity. The most successful football managers ask their players to express themselves as individuals but instil in them an understanding of exactly when to pass the ball to someone else. Good theatre directors ask actors to sound like Prince Hamlet one moment, an attendant lord the next.

'Democracy is a bad thing,' a Russian cellist once muttered to me rather ominously, and there are plenty of musicians who do not believe it works in an orchestral context. Some assume it is simply not possible for an orchestra to sound unanimous without some form of dictatorship. A few just don't want to take part in a process that demands more individual responsibility. But apathetic electorates get the leadership they deserve and although with a large orchestra there has to be a level of autocracy, subtle leadership and a positive response to it prevents the model from being so black and white. Conductors can yield to the flow of the room, and, as long as this is done with complete awareness, they will not lose any authority in doing so. A songbird will sing to its heart's content if it feels a hand is there to support it, an external sense of security giving both freedom and licence to its song.

*

If an emotional history of the orchestra is ever written, 11 March 1829 would prove to be a seminal date. On that evening Felix Mendelssohn conducted Bach's *St Matthew Passion* at the Berliner Singakademie. It was the first time this piece of music had been heard outside Bach's home town of Leipzig, and roughly a hundred years had passed since it had been composed. Up until that point the majority of concerts had been given either with the composer present or by musicians who would have felt completely at home with the style and language of whatever works they were playing. In many cases, the ink on the page was barely dry. The music was almost always contemporary, and consequently players could trust their own knowledge, experience, and taste. But when Mendelssohn stood up in front of the musicians in Berlin, not one of them would have known the piece, and perhaps only a few would have been familiar with any music by Bach whatsoever. They had no reference point for their opinions and looked to Mendelssohn, their conductor, to tell them, apparently rather strictly, how to play such intriguing music from the past.

Today the situation is reversed. It is when playing the music of our own time that orchestra musicians are most accepting of a conductor's opinions. It's contemporary music that orchestras don't know so well – the exact opposite of how it was two hundred years ago. The fact that nowadays the vast majority of all classical performances are of pieces known by the musicians puts enormous strain on the relationship between conductor and player. In all probability the orchestra will have performed the work more often than the conductor, yet it is the conductor's opinion that is expected to hold sway.

Playing in an orchestra is an extremely difficult job. The hours are irregular and anti-social; the physical demands are constant and often considerably uncomfortable; the choice of repertoire is beyond your control and repeated over and over again; and you normally sit next to the same person for many years, with rarely any opportunity for promotion. You have to express yourself, but not too much, and have a strong personality that you are expected to reveal only on demand. And in most countries you do all this for a barely sustainable salary and within a profession that is undervalued by society.

But the job is also a dream come true – an opportunity to be at the centre of some of the greatest achievements of human civilisation. To spend a lifetime with cultural giants such as Mozart, Beethoven, Brahms, Wagner, Verdi, Debussy, Stravinsky, Mahler, Strauss, is an incredible privilege. Although musicians are often compromised by circumstances beyond their control, deep down their commitment to striving for the best is strong. They would never have become good enough players to join an orchestra in the first place had they not had an uncommon dedication to music from an early age. Although the chances of being disappointed are not insignificant, the possibility is always there of taking part in a profound musical experience, and being part of sharing that experience with many others.

This is not a book about the ups and downs of orchestra life. Every player is far more qualified than me to write about that. But as a few years ago a survey of around fifteen hundred orchestra musicians revealed that over 70 per cent of them had suffered stress as a result of a conductor, the reality of the lives of the musicians we work with is not something that we should ignore. Conductors who were good enough instrumentalists to have started their professional lives playing in an orchestra are at a distinct advantage when it comes to understanding the psychology of an orchestra, but a natural human awareness and sensitivity can help make up for an absence of direct experience. We are in a position to make a considerable difference to the quality of the players' musical lives and this is a task that should be embraced very seriously.

In this sense we conduct the musicians, not the music.

They are the ones who make the sound, and if we can make them feel respected as people, and valued as players, the performance will be immeasurably better. Professionals will always deliver a basic standard that is somehow acceptable. But that is not a level of quality that sustains the art form. And no one aspires to that, especially not the musicians themselves. They didn't join an orchestra to be a professional. They joined to be a musician. They don't want to be bored. They want to be stretched and fulfilled. But no matter how ambitious every player is to maintain their own standard and curiosity, it is all but impossible for them to do so, day in day out, if they are being conducted by someone who isn't able to create, or doesn't understand, the conditions that that player's personal motivation needs and deserves. We all make choices in our lives and orchestra musicians are no less responsible for their personal happiness than anyone else, but the conductors who empathise with the instrumentalists' physical, musical, emotional, financial, professional, and personal challenges are going to get better results. We have a duty to lead the morale of the group. Creating and maintaining a positive morale is where the musical and human qualities of a conductor meet.

That is not to say that we cannot make significant demands on the orchestra. Quite the opposite. We must. A common frustration for players is that they sometimes do not feel they are being pushed enough and in its own way this is just as much a sign of disrespect as demanding too much. Orchestras want to achieve or even surpass their potential. A conductor needs to know what that level is, how to achieve it musically, and how to ask for it personally.

This is obviously much easier if you work regularly with the same musicians and there are many advantages to being an orchestra's music director or chief conductor. The days when such a position came with despotic power to hire and fire players have gone, but a certain legacy of the intensity in that relationship remains and players on the whole try their hardest for their 'boss'. They see the work they do together as their most important, both in terms of how they view themselves as well as how they want to be judged by the public. Music directors have first call on whatever financial funds are available, and so their repertoire is often the most adventurous of the season. The combination of absorbing programming and a broader long-term significance for the performances generates a self-motivated ambition within the orchestra that the conductor benefits from hugely. Shared experiences, in the same building, sometimes over many years, all contribute to the depth of musicianship everyone can express, and the mutual trust and respect that can grow during a fruitful relationship enables the highest of standards to be sought. Regular audience members expect the best of this relationship too. Superlatives become the acknowledged aim of everyone involved.

But familiarity can breed less positive outcomes as well. The chemistry that drew a conductor and orchestra together in the first place can lose its fizz over time. Players can become bored with their music director and disgruntled if they feel unable to play their best on a regular basis. It can also become hard for conductors to maintain an appropriate level of engagement with the players on a personal level. If you are too friendly with any of them, it can lead to accusations of favouritism; keeping your distance invites the criticism of appearing aloof. Such politics are distracting for everyone.

Guest conductors, on the other hand, know nothing whatsoever about the players. It's easy to treat everyone the same and this musically and personally egalitarian atmosphere can create a refreshing and positive working environment. Sometimes too much knowledge is a bad thing. If you know which musicians are having a difficult time either at work or at home, you might make a special effort to be sensitive to them. Yet this could be precisely when those players want to be treated as normally as possible. It's much easier for conductors not to overthink their requests if they know nothing of the orchestra's politics or its individual personalities. A certain ignorance works the other way round as well. Guest conductors can feel like a breath of fresh air to an orchestra, their novelty still burning bright, and, unlike music directors, they cannot be held responsible for any extra-musical issues the orchestra might be having to deal with at the time.

Although the personal challenges are easier for a guest conductor, the musical ones are harder. It can be difficult to second-guess the level everyone expects to reach and to raise the bar to an achievable limit when you are not sure where it normally lies. You don't know which musicians have the experience to improve something on their own or which sections of the orchestra will be grateful to you for taking that responsibility on yourself. Nor is there time to correct any miscalculation of the orchestra's learning curve. You have to earn and maintain the musicians' respect with every gesture, and you have to be musically credible whatever style of music you are conducting. There is simply no margin for error – a margin that most people need if they are to create something really special. Even when the performance is successful, a guest conductor's fulfilment can feel limited. There is little opportunity to make a deep connection with either the players or the audience.

A music directorship is a sort of marriage. It needs constant nurturing, and despite an ease of connection and many shortcuts in communication, nothing can be taken for granted. It can offer far more reward than the relative flippancy of a series of one-night stands. But both alternatives have their advantages – and some conductors are better suited to, and consequently enjoy more, one rather than the other.

★

Creativity is about connecting. The handshake between the conductor and the concertmaster at the start of each rehearsal or performance is an acknowledgement of that fact. In one sense it is simply a friendly and natural greeting, but it is also a convention that launches the idea that conductor and orchestra are going to embark on a journey together, a voyage concluded with a similar gesture, even if there might be differences of opinion as to whether the trip was any good or not.

The best concertmasters see their role as far more than the practical one of turning the conductor's gestures and ideas into a technical and musical reality. They engage in every aspect of the orchestra's life and lead the group's spirit as much as its performance. Their constant presence is meant to guarantee that the orchestra tries to maintain its standards, whatever the circumstances it finds itself in. In leading the sound, rhythm, and timing of the orchestra, the concertmaster is the first channel through which the conductor communicates. It is a pivotal relationship, one that ideally works both ways, for concertmasters are also responsible for communicating the orchestra's thoughts and feelings back to the conductor. A good concertmaster is able simultaneously to follow and lead, both artistically and psychologically, and it is not easy to find such delicate balance. They also have to be able to play the violin.

A positive, supportive, dedicated, and of course musically capable and aware concertmaster is an incalculable asset. While it's quite hard for orchestra players to take no notice of their conductor, it is almost impossible for them to ignore their concertmaster. When the orchestra senses a consonance between the two, a great many things fall effortlessly into place.

On a musical level, a conductor's engagement with each musician varies depending on the instrumentalist's role within the orchestra or the piece being played at the time. Richard Strauss said that a conductor should only ever conduct the strings, the woodwind should be treated like soloists, and if you so much as look at the brass they will just play too loudly. It is simplistic, but the principle is not completely misguided. Although looking at the brass during *The Ride of the Valkyries* is actually the best way to control their sonority, and a flautist would probably prefer to be encouraged than ignored during the well-known solo in *Carmen*, as far as I am concerned the string section is definitely the focal point of a conductor's energy and attention.

As members of the largest family of instruments in the orchestra, it is the string players who need the most physical encouragement, whether being implored to give more or persuaded to give less. It is human nature for sixty-odd people to doubt the individual significance of what they do in a group. To push each one of them to their limit, and to remind them of their importance, and the huge difference each one of them can make, is often a prime focus of the conductor in the most loud and passionate music. Conversely, in music of extreme tranquillity, you have to entice a string player not to take too much individual responsibility for the sound. This is much more difficult. It is technically harder to play quietly and it is emotionally more challenging too. Not feeling as if you are contributing to the expression can feel counter-intuitive. Even the word *ex*pression suggests something that moves out rather than in, and it is logical that musicians find it easier to express themselves playing louder than softer. A conductor can engender a *crescendo* with the slightest of invitations whereas a *diminuendo* needs considerably more powers of persuasion. There are plenty of fast and almost impossible notes in Wagner's *Tristan und Isolde,* but to express the whispered sensuality and vulnerable spirituality of the central love duet is the far greater achievement.

As a team within a team, string players appreciate that they need to be particularly unanimous. It is not their role to be independent, and though they need to give of themselves completely, no one player should ever stick out of the texture unless the composer has specifically asked for that to be the case. It is in an orchestral string player's nature to want to blend. Their mentality is to be a part of the greater sound. There is still individual responsibility, but it is relatively easy for a conductor to influence this without any implied criticisms being taken personally.

Whereas string players normally share a music stand with a colleague, and therefore somehow the personal responsibility too, every other musician in the orchestra has their own part, and though these are often doubled or even tripled elsewhere, the presence of an individual sheet of music in front of them can understandably lead to a more possessive connection to the work they are playing. There are musical advantages to this identification, but it can create psychological challenges for the conductor as well. Although you choose your words carefully, whomever you are addressing, it needs an extra sensitivity to talk to a potentially more egocentric cog within the orchestral machine.

Having said that, professional players are professional players and most probably prefer a direct approach to a time-consuming and convoluted one. Treating a problem with kid gloves can actually come across as a suggestion that the player might not be confident enough to handle any criticism. It depends on the players, but if they sound out of tune they might prefer just be told that is the case rather than listen to a conductor awkwardly beating about the bush with 'I was just wondering, if you might consider, possibly, maybe I am wrong, but the D sharp just sounds a shade under the note. It's probably just a question of colour, but perhaps you could try to play with a little more sense of optimistic brightness?' Of course, neither do they want to simply hear 'You're flat!' but the middle ground between these two extremes is not hard to find for anyone who seeks it.

It's not always a criticism to tell players they sound out of tune. On their own, they may not be. But the inner workings of musical harmony mean that every player needs to be constantly open and flexible to altering their own musical truth in order to make the chord work as a whole. Some woodwind sections like sorting this out on their own. Others prefer to let the conductor address it so that dealing with any of the internal personal politics involved is left to an outsider.

When it comes to the woodwind's individual contributions, or any player's solos for that matter, the conductor's main responsibility is to make sure that the rest of the orchestra is aware of the audible limelight these moments require. You can offer musical leadership of the solo, and most players are open and happy to tweak their own views if you make a good enough case for why, but these passages are the high point of the player's own performance, and you need to weigh up the pros and cons of involving yourself in how they should sound. Musicians will have come to a rehearsal with a strong opinion about their solos. Bassoonists might regard playing the highly exposed opening of Stravinsky's *The Rite of Spring* as one of the most important moments of their musical life. Similarly, a cor anglais player will have given a great deal of thought to the famous solo in Dvořák's

Symphony 'From the New World'. Every snare drum player has practised the beginning of Ravel's *Boléro* far more than any conductor will have studied it. Some players have to be encouraged to reveal more of their personality than they might think appropriate, whereas others might need to be persuaded of the value of a particular solo sounding as if it is being played in the third person. In certain circumstances, an emotional distance can bring even greater poignancy. You want to stimulate individuality, and a sense of ownership, but you have to make sure that this fits into the road map you think the piece should be following as a whole. Your overview of the structure is one that you hope can encompass any orchestral soloist's practical needs or musical desires.

One of the biggest challenges for brass players comes from so much of the music they play having been written for instruments that are quieter than the ones now in use. When a modern symphony orchestra plays music from the eighteenth and nineteenth centuries, the brass sections are constantly having to underplay their parts – not only the specific dynamic markings they see in front of them but also the emotional energy of the music itself. However aware of this they are, always keeping a lid on what they play can be exhausting and unfulfilling. Brass players don't want to drown out anyone else but it is often not their fault if they do, and it can be disheartening for them to feel they have to water down their sound in order to cope with a problem that is not of their making. You try to be sensitive to the patience this requires, couching your vocabulary in terms of colour rather than volume and avoiding excessive repetition of quantitative terms like 'less' or 'much less'.

After all, conductors wouldn't take kindly to consistently being asked to rein themselves in either.

Percussion players spend a lot of their time not playing at all. There is not much music written before the twentieth century that even needs them. But their coolness in coping with the pressure, as well as the boredom, of the long periods of inactivity that can precede crucial contributions never ceases to amaze me. Conductors do not have to count bars' rest. And it is a lot easier to be constantly involved. For instance, three hours separate cymbal crashes in a performance of Wagner's *Die Meistersinger von Nürnberg*, and an awareness and open acknowledgement of these musicians' longueurs can be a great help when calling on their musical support when you need it. If people think a conductor is in a position of power, that is nothing compared to the opportunities afforded a percussion section. They have louder sticks.

★

I do not mean to suggest that how a conductor interacts with the musicians is exclusively determined by which instruments they play. There are as many different temperaments in an orchestra as there are people, and the instrumental section each one belongs to simply provides the context for whatever specific communication is necessary. Players could equally well be categorised by how they like to work, and I don't think their preference for one particular conducting style over another is at all dependent on where they sit.

Most musicians spend much more of their lives rehearsing than performing. So, although the rehearsals are obviously not as important as the concerts themselves, it is healthy if they can be fulfilling on their own terms. Having said that, there's no guarantee that a stimulating preparation process will always result in the best performances, while a tedious approach can sometimes produce surprisingly wonderful concerts. One or two of the most respected conductors have even been renowned for the boredom of their rehearsals.

The relative significance of the rehearsal totally depends on the type of orchestra involved. An amateur orchestra is clearly voluntary and in some cases its members even pay to play. When I started conducting the Edgware Symphony Orchestra (my first job, in fact) I quickly realised that if we finished before the scheduled end of the rehearsal the players were disappointed not to be getting their money's worth. Although the enthusiasm was heartening, it was not the best way to begin to understand a professional orchestra's psyche. Amateurs don't need motivating. They simply need a structure within which to fulfil their passion; an outlet for their love of music. They have a very particular set of priorities.

Professionalism is a double-edged quality. I love the adeptness of professional orchestras to solve any musical problems that come their way, and admire their reliability under often intense pressure. But professionalism itself is a dangerous goal, and, unless seen as a means to an end, can camouflage a fear of failure that prevents the greatest success. The football manager Luiz Felipe Scolari told his

Brazilian team to 'feel more amateur than professional'. They won the World Cup. The professionalism necessary to achieve the highest results can suffocate the amateur-defining love for something that is ultimately what communicates so much to others.

The words 'professional' and 'amateur' used to have different resonances. A hundred years ago amateurs were respected individuals, whereas the word 'professional' was a derogatory term. Nowadays 'amateurish' can imply casual and incapable, while 'professional' is a significant compliment. But Oscar Wilde's quip about amateur musicians being an example of all men killing the thing they love is unfair. Their commitment and zest adds to the music's life and purpose, and the variety of professions they represent supplies a rich hinterland to its expression. As is often pointed out, it was amateurs who built the Ark, and professionals who built the *Titanic*. But, financial considerations aside, the two worlds need not be mutually exclusive. Professionals can maintain an amateur's enthusiasm and spirited freedom, and it's possible for amateurs to approach performances with the concentration and reliability of professionals. A conductor establishes the conditions for both these things and the best of both worlds is not a bad aspiration to have, whoever you are working with.

Unlike amateurs, students normally have to play in an orchestra as part of their education. But they are usually excited to learn, and thrilled to be playing the standard repertoire for the first time. Their exuberant anticipation of what lies ahead of them is extremely infectious, and high-level youth orchestras have given me many of the most memorable experiences of my life. Inevitably, when conducting a student orchestra, you become as much a teacher as you are a conductor, and some conductors find this educational role a more comfortable fit than others. It can be incredibly rewarding to help young people unearth more of their ability than they might have realised they had, and it is a privilege to be the one who accompanies them into the kind of emotional discovery that, for example, the first playing of a Mahler symphony can unlock. With nothing to lose, with no consciousness of the possibility of failure, they live on the wild side of the music, they embrace the edge, and countenance no compromise. Although they are unaware of it, their innocent wonder at the extraordinary power of music can be a reminder to their conductor of just what a special life it is. The 'teacher' gets just as much out of it as the student.

It can be very fulfilling when young musicians play exactly what you ask of them, and do so with complete conviction and pride, but as a group they are rarely able to give you more than that. The success of the concert is limited by what you demand. Extensive rehearsals often allow those demands to be substantial but there is still a cut-off point defined by a single conductor's view. Even the very best youth orchestras make me realise that the musical tension that can accompany the relationship between a professional orchestra and conductor need not be a bad thing. Often this form of constructive friction leads to performances being more than the sum of their parts.

Sadly, surveys show that the gap between student idealism and professional reality for orchestra musicians is the largest for any profession. Indeed, many lay the blame for this at the feet of conductors. We are accused of having inspired the student only then to peg back the professional. There are many factors involved, however, and though conductors must take their share of responsibility, it is too simplistic to suggest it is all our fault. I suspect that both the fantasy and the actuality are equally problematic. But we should never be tempted to dampen the exuberant optimism of youth. The reality of compromise shatters every dream.

★

The first time you work with an orchestra you have absolutely no idea what to expect. I rather enjoy the freedom of the unknown. But it does mean there is a limit to how far you can plan your rehearsal. I have learned not to be taken aback when something I thought would be simple proves difficult or a passage I expected to be very complicated rapidly sorts itself out. I once conducted Beethoven's Ninth Symphony with an orchestra that had not played the piece for over a decade. For no particular reason it had just slipped through their programming net. The absence of any communal expectations meant that certain things were easier than normal, but many other challenges made me realise how valuable those expectations are. Experience has taught me how to deal with surprises but I cannot say it has led to fewer of them.

A lot depends on what an orchestra considers its cultural identity to be. A group famous for how effortlessly it navigates modern music will take a piece like Harrison

Birtwistle's *Earth Dances* in its stride. One renowned for Wagner will not blink at the complexities of *The Ring*. But swap the repertoire over and an institutional uncertainty can affect what the orchestra finds hard and what it does not. On an individual level, a good musician can play Messiaen's *Turangalîla-Symphonie* just as well as Mozart's 'Jupiter', but conductors do not conduct individual musicians; we conduct the group. It is the self-belief of the orchestra as a whole that sets the speed at which any problems are resolved.

Musicians look to the conductor to help them do just that. Some players believe that is all a conductor is there for. Some think there would be fewer problems without one. But as much as conductors disagree with the extremes of both those views, you cannot cherry-pick the parts of the job you enjoy the most. You might dream of simply expressing the music with some kind of perfect orchestral machine, but fortunately such a virtual reality does not exist. Our role is indeed to help the musicians play together, well balanced, and in tune, and though rolling up our sleeves and getting on with such practicalities might seem tedious, that's what the job is. Or at least a significant part of it. How quickly you can hear something that is wrong, pinpoint its cause, and identify a solution is what determines how much time you have left to seduce the musicians with the spiritual profundity of your fantasy and your deeply rooted inner connection with the composer!

Joking aside, how you balance what is with what you'd like it to be does matter and you spend much of your life negotiating between the two. The aim is to combine both without compromising either but inevitably one always falls a little to one side or the other. Whatever level you are working at, imagining a limit to what can be accomplished easily creates a barrier of considerable significance, but on the other hand there is no point striving for an ideal that is unachievable. If you can determine as soon as possible where that tipping point lies there is no reason why anyone should feel that they have failed purely because of someone else's definition of what failure means. Knowing where to set the goalposts, doing so early on, and then sticking to where they are is crucial for a sense of satisfaction that it is human nature to desire. It seems to be a common trait that large groups of people are reluctant to give their all unless forced or inspired to do so by someone or something else. A conductor has to encourage orchestra musicians to achieve more than they thought possible on their own. But if, in trying to do so, we push them past the point at which they can no longer express themselves, this very soon results in a downward spiral in confidence and enjoyment.

Much depends on how many rehearsals there are. But the quality of the orchestra's attitude to the work is probably more important than the quantity of time you have available. In that sense how much you accomplish is due as much to the players' ambition as it is to the conductor's. When everyone in the room feels equally responsible, many things can be achieved astonishingly quickly.

The danger of too little rehearsal time is that the stress of not feeling prepared can undermine one's ability to perform at one's best. A musician's tension is not the same as the music's intensity and the line between spontaneity and unpredictability is a narrow one. Uncertainty can have players on the edge of their seats, but that does not mean it will have the same effect on the audience.

Too much rehearsal is also problematic. It is comforting to feel as if one can solve every problem, highlight every detail, discover every colour, agree every dynamic, but only the biggest personalities can maintain their own adrenalin, let alone that of others, to sustain highly intensive work over a long period of time. The more rehearsal there is, the greater the likelihood of a concert that seeks only to recreate in public what has been achieved in private. Over-rehearsing can stifle genuine creativity during the performance and it is definitely possible to practise yourself away from the music. There comes a point at which you lose more than you gain. Knowing when that has been reached takes a combination of instinct and confidence. Experience teaches you that ending a rehearsal early won't necessarily be seen as a sign of laziness or a cheap attempt to gain popularity. Nor will working right up to the last available second be considered pedantic or futile if the musical advantages of doing so are clear to everyone involved.

However much or little rehearsal there is, you are always trying to create a sense of journey within the process, planning to improve constantly without peaking too soon. Pacing the rehearsals well, especially if they take place over several days, is comforting to the musicians and can make a big difference to the quality of the performance.

Most of the time, most of the orchestra will have played most of the music many, many times before. And with the most standard repertoire, it doesn't take long for players to feel as if they have tried every single request a conductor has ever made. You cannot set out to shed new light on a well-known work for its own sake, as the result will simply sound contrived and eccentric. However, if your vision does reveal a fresh approach to the players, it will feel equally vibrant to the audience. Ninety-nine per cent of the time the most popular works are indeed the greatest masterpieces of the repertoire. Beethoven's 'Pastoral' Symphony is a supreme example of its kind. In this category, there are no boring pieces, only boring performances – and a conductor is in a position to help an orchestra remember that.

Deeply connected to the interest or otherwise of the rehearsal process is the question of how often conductors should speak and what they should say when they do. Rehearsals establish a communication that can function without recourse to words. But, especially at the start of the rehearsal process, when a more physical connection might not yet have been established, some ideas are more efficiently expressed verbally. I think players accept being told, rather than just shown, what you would like to hear, if they feel that that is saving time rather than wasting it. It is what you actually say that matters.

Verbal requests are essentially either practical or imaginative. There are some musicians who just want to know if you want them to play louder, softer, longer, shorter, slower, or faster. Their pragmatism doesn't want their time squandered, or imagination insulted, by you suggesting they should try to sound like a lonely, love-sick Italian rose on a rainy afternoon in May. For every player who finds your similes thoughtful, amusing, poetic, specific, and relevant, there will be others who think they are pretentious

self-indulgence – or words to that effect, and more importantly a restriction on the scope of the musical gesture, and
their own expression of it. You often hear people say that
words cannot explain their feelings. Language can indeed
inhibit the complexity at the source of highly emotional
situations. But words force musicians to be creative in their
response to them, and those who enjoy taking a greater
ownership of the expression appreciate being allowed to
do so. Knowing your 'audience' and being aware of how
your comments are being received makes a big difference,
particularly if you are working in a foreign country.

I suspect today's musicians sound a lot more alike than
they did a hundred years ago. Recordings are easily available, young people frequently study abroad, and an abundance of international youth orchestras allows for a far
greater exchange of ideas at a crucial stage in a musician's
development than ever used to be the case. But put a hundred cosmopolitan players into an orchestra and as a group
their national characteristics still reveal themselves with
all the stereotypical differences of that particular country's
identity. These are generalisations, but it is hard not to be
aware of the work ethic of the Japanese, the suave style of
the Italians, the passion of the Hungarians, the efficiency of
the Americans, the sophistication of the Swedes, the teamwork of the Dutch, the freedom of the South Americans,
the cultural confidence of the Germans, the 'no-worries'
attitude of the Australians, and the more-passionate-than-
we-like-to-admit British. Music might be an international
language but it is one full of many different accents and
dialects.

Having said that, the cultures of all who play Western orchestral music are strikingly similar. Mozart and Beethoven might have been at the forefront of globalisation but there are plenty of places on the planet that remain completely untouched by their music. Although I have clocked up my fair share of air miles, I have yet to work anywhere that felt especially unusual. The symphonic and operatic world is a much smaller one than we like to imagine.

I would not say that I adjust my musicianship to connect with an orchestra's culture. I believe there is a right sound and style for each composer and, while taking into account the identity of the orchestra, hope broadly to recreate them wherever I go. But the means of achieving your view varies hugely from country to country. Ending a rehearsal too soon in one place is as bad as using every minute of it in another. Whereas you might need to draw more emotion out of an orchestra's discipline in one city, you could find yourself having to encourage greater focus within the fervent free-range expression of another. The fact that your personality is likely to be better suited to one rather than another is perhaps the main reason why some conductors work better with particular groups than with others. Personally, I enjoy creating order out of passion more than the other way around.

I used to conduct an orchestra in Sweden quite often. I was particularly fond of one of the woodwind players who always nodded his head in voracious agreement with everything I said. After several years of working together, our paths crossed in a backstage corridor for the first time. It was only then, in trying to start up a conversation with him, that I realised he didn't speak a word of English. I was somewhat embarrassed not to have seen through his brilliant deflecting mechanism for coping with more attention from me in rehearsal than he probably thought appropriate for his playing.

There are other challenges in working abroad. Humour can be a most valuable tool in creating and maintaining a positive atmosphere, and it is a very effective way of defusing tension. Disguising criticism with a cloak of self-deprecation can produce the right results while making sure the air stays free of any potential negativity. But you have to be careful. Not everybody's sense of humour is the same. A joke in Manchester might not go down so well in Munich and what could be considered a light touch in Paris might well be thought of as superficial in St Petersburg.

The main reason for not talking in rehearsal is that while you are talking, you cannot be listening. Solzhenitsyn's remark that 'the less you talk, the more you hear' was politically loaded but as a philosophy it is no less relevant to conductors. Orchestras know when they are not being listened to and, when that is the case, understandably feel that whatever they play is an irrelevance to the conductor's pre-planned agenda. Listening is the most important thing a conductor should ever do. This might seem obvious but it isn't as easy as it sounds. Inexperienced conductors will be so determined to impart their view of how the music goes that they won't be open to how the orchestra is actually playing. It is quite hard to give and receive at exactly the same moment and if you add in the stress of a novel and potentially intimidating situation, young conductors can easily get to the end of a rehearsal and realise, if they are honest with themselves, that they have absolutely no idea what it really sounded like. Of course you hear what is being played. But listening is different. It is an attitude – intellectually active rather than physiologically passive.

Only by truly listening can we know what we think about what we hear. From that flow the most basic questions a conductor has to answer in front of the orchestra. Do I like it? Could I grow to like it? Should I change it? Can I change it? Was it the result of something I did? The time it takes to rehearse is directly related to a musical certainty and speed of thought in deciding how or whether to respond to the orchestra if what we hear differs from what we want to achieve.

★

The fact that it is simply not practical for musicians in an orchestra to play from the full score means that only the conductor has access to all the information at any one time. In pieces that players know well this isn't especially significant but given the importance of how musical lines relate to one another, the comprehensive knowledge that the score provides is crucial in showing how each part intertwines with, and around, another. And it is what the players do not have in their own parts that they most need a conductor for. Each instrument contributes to the musical line only some of the time. Lacing their voices in and out of the various sections of the orchestra, establishing their connections, and projecting them above a more general backdrop of colour and harmony is how the conductor releases a perspective that listeners need in order to follow the musical story.

Rehearsing is about coming to an agreement with the musicians about which of them has the leading role and when. This is not necessarily simply the part that should be most audible to the audience; it is more a question of realising who is in charge at any one time. It is rather like trying to keep a ball in the air as it passes around the orchestra. The conductor sets the ball in motion but from then on the responsibility for keeping it 'in play' is constantly shifting from group to group, player to player, reverting to the conductor only in situations where the ball might not be 'audible' to everyone else. There can be circumstances, normally acoustic ones, in which it is in fact better for the players to agree not to listen, at which point the conductor's responsibility does indeed become more specific and practical. But, most of the time, our own listening is as much trained on the ball as the players' is. Figuratively speaking, the baton is passed around the orchestra. A conductor almost always gets the music going, but once up and running there should be a feeling that you are constantly accompanying the musicians as much as leading them. In that sense the joke that a conductor is someone who can follow many people at once is at least half the story.

Beethoven's Third Symphony begins with two loud and arresting chords. A conductor cannot shirk the need to make these sound unanimous. But by the time you get to the third bar, the second violins and violas have to play a rhythmic *ostinato* the constancy of which is up to them to maintain. It is then your job to make sure that the cellists who are playing the melody keep up with this inner pulse before handing over their line to the first violins. At this point the accompaniment becomes less articulated, enabling a little more freedom in the music should that be considered appropriate. In the space of a dozen bars, the musical and practical leadership of the symphony has passed from the conductor to the accompaniment to the melody. An ever-shifting of responsibility is what makes an orchestra a living, breathing body, all of whose organs are working all the time yet only one of which is perceived as being the most important at any given moment.

★

In some ways a conductor is a sort of musical satnav. You have a course of direction in mind when you start but if players take a turning you were not expecting you will need to know whether to recalibrate your route or tell them to turn around where possible. The more often you conduct a piece, the more you realise the variety of different routes that can be taken. One might assume that over time a conductor's opinions become entrenched but, in my experience at least, I find the opposite to be true. When you start conducting it is easy to believe that your musical conviction forms the basis of your right to conduct at all and that your authority stems from your musical certainty. The stronger your ideas, the stronger your leadership. You are aware that as much as players don't particularly enjoy being told what you want them to do, it is far more annoying for them *not* to be told what you want them to do. But as your experience with a particular work increases, you realise that there are more options than you might have first thought, and you develop a view of the piece that includes a range of opinions without any loss of distinction. In fact, because you are able to take on board more of the players' instincts, this actually strengthens its power. That's why conductors get better as they get older. Not because they become *more* sure about what it is they want to achieve but because they grow to understand how wide a masterpiece's interpretative parameters can be. Your own belief system becomes a broader church – one within which most players feel happier expressing themselves – and you don't need necessarily to order a U-turn every time you hear something surprising.

A young conductor's 'do it my way' approach can come across as arrogance but more often than not I suspect it is probably the result of a *lack* of confidence. Trusting the musicality of your players starts with trusting yourself, and that can take time. And experience also teaches you to trust your skill as a conductor as well as your purely musical ability. You realise that there's no need to rehearse something again if you know that you can improve it yourself without saying anything in advance of the next time you play it. You learn what will get better on its own, or what needs direct attention, and players respect it when they can see that you are looking for a solution internally before you start asking them to make the change themselves.

It is not exactly rocket science to point out that how we talk to orchestras contributes significantly to the dynamic of the relationship we have with them. You don't need to read a book on conducting to know that people would rather not be shouted at, that most of us respond better to encouragement than to negativity, and that criticism framed by positivity is far more likely to be successful than impatience, rudeness, or anger. But flattery isn't the answer either. Too much praise can turn a large group off, or make an individual so self-conscious about a particularly special moment that it becomes robbed of its sincerity in performance. Orchestras know the quality of their work. An honest, even generous appreciation from the conductor is welcome but if players are ever told they are sounding better than they are, it makes them think that the conductor is deaf, insincere, or both. Excessive praise can almost be as unhelpful as constant criticism. Almost. People would still rather be told that they are too good than that they are too bad. The best approach is to concentrate on what you want and not what you don't want. The former feels musical, the latter more a personal confrontation. Renovation is normally quicker than demolition and reconstruction.

Conductors spend a lot of time in rehearsal telling players what they think, while players spend a lot of their breaks in rehearsal telling each other what they think. There might be practical or emotional advantages to this, but such an imbalance is not particularly healthy. Orchestra musicians have long been disempowered from speaking their mind within the traditional structure of the rehearsal process, and these still clearly delineated lines are not easy to cross. Some feel more comfortable with the formality of this conventional grid and with the protection that its barriers afford. There is an undoubted efficiency that accompanies a more dictatorial approach. Yet conductors who see the benefits of a modern and democratic environment encourage players to voice their opinions freely. If done with respect and tact, a sense of two-way traffic relaxes the atmosphere in the room enormously. There is also the possibility that a player's idea is a better one, blasphemous as that might sound.

★

Tension in a rehearsal is sometimes based on a lack of appreciation by both the conductor and the player that the other might be nervous. Both 'sides' tend to presume that the other is supremely confident. This is often not the case and an awareness of the potential anxiety of others is a useful sensitivity for everyone to have. Conductors should never underestimate the challenges both they and the music itself set the players, and in particular the peer pressure that those challenges can create within the orchestra. There is usually only ever one conductor in a rehearsal room, and though there is no shortage of people judging you, it's not quite the same thing as a violinist having to play a solo in front of thirty other violinists, however supportive those colleagues might be. An orchestra plays a significant part in setting the tone of the room, but the conductor is in a position to steer its emotional temperature towards something intense enough to inspire but sufficiently relaxed to allow the musicians to feel emotionally at ease with a piece's difficulty. No player ever makes a mistake on purpose and how a conductor reacts to one can be significant in helping prevent it from happening again. Too much of a grimace and a tension around the moment can linger. Too much of a smile and it can seem as if you don't care. How we react to our own mistakes matters too.

John Wayne thought that apologising was a sign of weakness, but cowboy conductors don't do so well, and acknowledging a slip is more often a sign of strength. Up to a point. Own up to every single one of them and you start to erode your authority. Players like their conductor to be self-effacing, but they also always know when a mistake has been made, so if you can in some way show that you know too, most musicians will be forgiving. Maybe not endlessly so, but people are patient enough for it to be far better to admit your sins than to act as if they didn't happen. That is then just doubly insulting.

It is said that you have no right to call yourself an experienced conductor until you have conducted a very soft chord very loudly. (It tends to be conductors who say this.) But although we are not regularly exposed by such right or wrong scenarios – most of our errors are musical or psychological misjudgements – the potential for 'wrong notes' is still there, and the most audible of these often occur during concertos, where the responsibility for accompanying a soloist changes our role into something more specific. Players must enjoy seeing our brows furrow and sweat beads appear as a pianist approaches the end of the last-movement cadenzas in Beethoven's Fourth Piano Concerto. With a solid orchestral sound having seamlessly to take over from the fluidity of the soloist's scales at precisely the right moment, all the performers are conscious that for once the conductor has nowhere to hide and should the cue be given either too late or too early, it will indeed be immediately apparent. To have to show definite intent despite not being in complete control of the situation can be stressful. 'Welcome to our world,' the players would say. Quite.

Conducting can be intensely demanding on both musical and psychological levels but when it comes to anything more physically tiring, what we have to do is nothing compared to even the most straightforward things the music asks of the players. I am often conscious of the ease of waving a stick around while the musicians in front of me have to move in often very repetitive and uncomfortable, and always predetermined, ways. The stamina they need, quite apart from the skill, is extraordinary. Conductors can essentially move however much or little we want to, and being able to choose our gestures, albeit within reason, is considerably less taxing than having them forced on you. I might be mentally drained after conducting a Mahler symphony or a Wagner opera but rarely am I physically worn out. Freedom of movement is liberating not burdensome, and being able to be in charge of what should be a natural physicality anyway makes an enormous difference. Conversely, there are not many things more exhausting than playing the second violin part of *The Marriage of Figaro*.

★

An important art for a conductor in rehearsal is knowing when to let go. When is it good enough? What does 'good enough' mean anyway? Good enough for the orchestra?

Good enough for the conductor? Good enough for the audience? Good enough for the music?

There are various reasons why a passage might not be improving in rehearsal. It is possible that its demands exceed the capabilities of the orchestra. It is equally possible that the conductor's ideas about that section are not appropriate and that an orchestra's inability to play them is not born out of reluctance or limited skill but simply from the fact that the musical idea doesn't support the request in the first place. Trying to push a square peg into a round hole is never going to work, and a problem in rehearsal can be a sign that conductors should look to themselves to resolve. But whatever the reason for a lack of progress, moving on need not be an admission of failure. A dog's reluctance to relinquish a bone is more unhealthy for the dog than it is for the bone.

To call someone a perfectionist is nowadays not necessarily a compliment. It might have once been intended as praise, but contemporary psychology more often links it with words such as 'obsessive' and 'controlling'. Musicians engage with perfection every day. Outside nature, there are not many things more perfect than Brahms's Fourth Symphony and it is understandable that we should want to honour that perfection by attempting to mirror it in our performances. But not everybody wants that challenge. 'It'll be fine' is a discouragingly unambitious attempt at reassurance. 'Fine' is not good enough. It is not what we are asking an audience to give time and money to hear. Classical music is much more than 'fine' and we constantly seek performances in which the aspiration matches that of the piece we are playing. But the greatest pieces constantly raise the bar of what you hope to achieve and you need the humility to recognise that there can come a point at which striving for perfection impedes our ability to express it. As current business jargon aptly puts it, 'Better' is the enemy of 'Good'.

There are some conductors who like to rehearse with the constant intensity of performance. They believe that this extra 10 per cent is the most important 10 per cent, and the more often you rehearse without it, the more it becomes an acceptable option for the music. They think pushing for 110 per cent is the only way of guaranteeing 100 per cent. But searching for the impossible can never be satisfying, and the risk of switching players off or forcing them to burn out is very real. More relaxed, or trusting, conductors feel that this extra 10 per cent will come on its own, and should not be demanded too often. Many musicians want to save their best for a paying public. 'I have only a certain number of high notes in me,' a tenor once said to me. 'I can't afford to waste any in rehearsals.'

A Russian conductor once cancelled a concert because he thought the playing in the final rehearsal had been so perfect that such a musical achievement could never be recreated. But such self-absorption is unusual. Public performances are the most important part of a conductor's professional life. They are, after all, the purpose of what we do. In many ways I find them the easiest part of the job. You hope always to motivate and inspire an orchestra, but whereas motivation is a people skill you need in rehearsals, the source of the inspiration in the performance is the music itself. The public nature of a concert is normally sufficient motivation for orchestra musicians, and for the conductor, free from a psychological obligation to keep the players engaged in rehearsal, it can be a relief to be able to concentrate purely on the inspiration of the music. Having only to express yourself as a musician on the stage can be a lot easier than having to do so as a personality in the re-hearsal room too.

It is also liberating to know that in a concert, unless something is very wrong indeed, you are not going to stop before the end of the piece. The length of the experience is down to the composer, not the conductor. No longer do you have to engage in the psychology of how to rehearse, whether to stop, or what to say. So much mental energy is spent in rehearsals thinking about whether something you just heard should be praised, criticised, rehearsed, or left alone. You constantly ask yourself if there is time to do a certain bit again. And if there is, whether that is the best use of the time or not. As T. S. Eliot's Prufrock would wonder: 'In a minute there is time/For decisions and revi-sions which a minute will reverse.' It is easy to spend a lot of energy analysing the past and worrying about the future, despite knowing that the most creatively influential place to be is in the present.

Performances allow you the joy of focusing on the pres-ent the entire time. You control the pacing of the music and therefore need a view of where you are heading, but a consciousness of musical time is not the same thing as feeling pressured by the intransigence of a rehearsal-room clock. Ending a rehearsal on time is easy. But getting to the

end of the music at the same moment as the end of the rehearsal, and doing so with a sense of accomplishment that
makes everyone feel good about themselves takes awareness and forethought, especially as you have no real idea
how long any orchestra might take to solve a problem you
set it. You are still in charge in a performance, of course,
but no longer do you have a responsibility for the practicalities of a player's professional life. Unlike the rehearsal,
it is now much clearer that you conduct the music and not
the musicians.

That is not to say that in performance you have no duty
towards the players at all. They look to you for musical
inspiration and rely on you to provide a solid and comfortable foundation for them to express themselves. Some
players want one more than the other but I would say most
want a combination of the two – a combination that I find
easier to achieve when not distracted by the mental clut-
ter that can easily build up inside you during the rehearsal
process itself.

Some musicians prefer rehearsals to paint a piece's big
picture with broad brushes, leaving details and practicalities for individuals to sort out alone. They simply want
to know the emotional temperature you believe the music should have. How much 'hotter' is Mahler than Sibe-
lius? Do you think Brahms should sound closer to Dvořák
or Beethoven? Is Mozart's musical personality romantic
or classical? They feel that if this sort of leadership is unequivocal they are capable and experienced enough players
for everything else to fall into place. But there are others
who like the specific building blocks of a performance to

be really clear, precisely so that they are freer to reveal a long-sighted view of the work in the concert. Their confidence in public comes from establishing secure foundations in private and they want to use the rehearsals to create a technical safety net that can encourage the sort of high-wire risks that need to be taken to deliver something exceptional when it matters.

A performance has to be more than the fruits of the rehearsal's labours. It should be something creative in its own right. This is what makes the audience feel as if it is witnessing something special: an intense and extreme experience that embraces the risk of sounding 'on the edge' without crossing a line that simply makes them uncomfortable. But risking failure is an important prerequisite for ultimate success and it can be dangerous to play safe. It is easier to swim if you are in the deep end of a pool.

A businessman once said to me that his success was down to his willingness to take risks but that he did so only when he knew they would pay off. A conductor is in a similar position to gauge the percentages. It is easy to sense when all the musicians in the orchestra are playing as one, listening to each other with an engagement that imperceptibly adjusts to the slightest unpremeditated *rubato*. Or to the biggest. It is a connection that can take anything in its stride, a stride stretched without effort, or shrunk without stress. In such situations, when you and the orchestra are so in sync that anything is possible, there is a danger of being tempted to exploit this freedom for its own sake; you need a certain discipline to trust that just because the orchestra is allowing you to be spontaneous, doing so will not always be an improvement. If simply being surprising is the goal, it's more impressive to pull a rabbit out of a hat.

Orchestras who play without conductor can do so very well. They can rehearse for long enough to agree a unified vision, take ownership of their responsibility for listening, and feel sufficiently self-motivated not to need someone else to push them to their limits. But it's very hard for them to take risks. The joke that says a conductor is like a condom – safer with but better without – seems to me to be a misunderstanding of a situation in which the exact opposite is true. The presence of an individual leader can allow far more freedom for a group than could otherwise be the case. Conductors can encourage others to take risks because they are there to catch them should that risk not come off. Although the original role of conductors was to keep musicians strictly together, enabling a freedom that allows them to drift apart occasionally is far more interesting.

*

Some conductors feel they can meet all their responsibilities in performance more easily if they are conducting without a score. The intensity of communication is increased by a constancy of eye-to-eye contact, as well as a full-bodied physicality undivided and undiluted by the barrier of the music stand. Not having to engage in the rather prosaic practicality of turning pages allows your arms the maximum opportunity to shape the music. The concentration of memory also forces you to keep hold of the musical line more attentively yourself, and the mindfulness this requires makes it easier not to be distracted by anything that is superfluous to the experience. Not having anything to read gives you more headspace to listen, and your heightened antennae make it easier to adjust instantly to anything the players might do and remain open to anything spontaneous that you hope might occur.

More metaphorically, a musician's job is to release the music from the limitations of its notation and free the notes from the two-dimensional prison of their five-lined printed cage. If music exists in any specific form at all, it does so in its published form. But the essence of music is not a physical reality. Musicians turn one into the other. For some, this job is simpler if all the dots, dashes, lines, curves, words, and symbols can be removed from the mind's eye. The variety of music's infinite colours is easier to imagine away from the black-and-white nature of their visual representation, and the structure of a composition becomes clearer when it can be 'pictured' not as a journey across the printed page but as a single event in a timeless space. Not having the music in front of you widens your vision and supports a more macroscopic view. Some people always conduct from memory, others never do, but for many of us our choice depends on the piece itself. The absence of a score can be liberating, but with complex and unfamiliar works, not having one might just be inhibiting.

There is always a heightened sense of drama when the players and audience notice that the conductor has chosen to 'go solo'. As long as the conductor feels no danger, I don't think a perception of risk is any bad thing. However, players know immediately if the conductor's decision has been motivated by vanity rather than musicianship. It is then easy for them to begrudge the extra responsibility forced on them, and instead of feeling free, open, and trusted, they go into survival mode, thus engaging less rather than more in what the conductor is showing.

Even when the motives are positively musical, the decision to do away with the score separates the conductor from the orchestra in a way that is problematic. Soloists are expected to play from memory, partly to distinguish themselves in some subliminal way from the other musicians on stage. They are meant to stand out from the crowd. The emotional, musical, technical, and even theatrical differences between the individual and the group are the point of the concerto as a form. But a purely orchestral piece is not about the conductor. You are not part of the story. Performing from memory turns a conductor into a kind of soloist, an actor on the stage. It separates us from the rest of the musicians, singling us out in a way that highlights the conductor as a 'leader' rather than a 'leader with'. In creating a personal narrative for the audience that is irrelevant to the musical experience, both the orchestra and the composer can feel neglected – if not during the performance, at least during the ensuing applause. Over the years this has had profound consequences for the image of the conducting profession as well as for the music industry as a whole.

Nietzsche remarked that 'many a man fails as an original thinker simply because his memory is too good'. The implication of this for conductors is that if you conduct from memory you will always give the same performance. That might be true if you have memorised your performance at the same time as memorising the score. But the opposite can also be the case. Without the score in front of you, far from having to be repetitive, this extra freedom has the potential to produce unique results every time. Of course, there is always more to discover in a score, and that process need never stop. The question is whether you are better able to generate an exciting response to a new observation with the score or without it, as well as how much perspective you are able to muster to understand which spur-of-the-moment choices will affect the experience as a whole.

I always react rather diffidently when I am congratulated on conducting from memory. Although I would have put time into that part of the process, it isn't the hardest aspect of the job by any means, and it can be disconcerting to feel that my memory is the talking point rather than the musical performance itself. I sometimes reply that I'm glad that at least the orchestra is using its music. This is partly a deflective quip, but it is relevant in the sense that I would never conduct a concerto or an opera without a score. With soloists or singers almost certainly performing from memory themselves, the potential for things to go awry is significantly greater than it is with orchestra players, and the risk of the performance not being able to recover from a perilous situation is made exponentially greater if the conductor is also 'scoreless'. Although orchestra musicians are capable of getting lost and would hope the conductor would be in a position to put things right, having the music in front of them means that the sort of mistakes they can make are quite clearly defined, and as such relatively easy for the conductor, or indeed the player, to correct.

And because the mentality of an individual within a group is conscious that in a specific sense there is less margin for error, orchestra players employ a different sort of concentration from that of soloists. As a result things go wrong amazingly rarely. Nevertheless, if I ever felt I would have to be able to look at the score myself in order to come to the rescue, I would always choose to use one.

If my preparation has given me the confidence to handle a work's more pragmatic necessities from memory without feeling distracted by the specific concentration that that requires, I find the freedom of conducting without looking at the printed music exhilarating. I feel closer to the composer, and in a way to the orchestra as well. I feel more connected. I love the subjectivity it offers me too, and to feel so at one with the music is deeply fulfilling. Conductors need to share their love for the music with those who are playing it, and it is easy to underestimate how open one has to be to do that. Speaking personally, I find that openness more accessible if I am conducting without a score. For all sorts of reasons, conducting by heart, which is a far healthier way of describing it than 'from memory', forces me to express myself more, and therefore, I hope, better. And if you conduct by heart, it doesn't really matter whether the score is in front of you or not.

Memory can be a distorting tool. And it is more reliable if your system for learning a score is one of trying to understand it rather than remember it. Once you understand something, it is impossible to forget it. It is also a far more positive, stimulating, and meaningful way to prepare. Because whatever physical control or psychological intuition conductors may have, it is your relationship with the music that lies at the heart of your artistic identity: you are a musician first, a conductor second.

3

Conducting Music

Life is the art of drawing sufficient conclusions
from insufficient premises.
Samuel Butler

There is no point being a messenger without a message. For conductors, this message is the result of the relationships you make with the composers whose music you perform. They vary depending on the composers of course, and like all relationships they change over time as much you do yourself. A strong connection you have with certain composers when you are young might wane as you get older. There are others whose musical aesthetic you grow into. I am profoundly embarrassed to own up to remembering a time when I did not like the music of Brahms. Yet now he is probably the composer who fulfils me most as a musician. And, who knows, there might even be a time when I feel I understand Berlioz. Some music has an adolescent quality; some pieces are more spiritual. That's not to say you need to be the same emotional age as the music to conduct it well. There are old conductors who have never lost their youthful adrenalin, while some young ones seem wise beyond their years.

I have been conducting a few of my favourite works for nearly thirty years now. And there must be some octogenarian conductors who have been performing certain pieces for over twice that length of time. To me, the Tenth

Symphonies of Mahler and Shostakovich feel like cousins I meet up with every year and, unlike actors who can play only roles that suit their age, the relationship you have with the music you conduct regularly is a lifelong collaboration that touches different parts of your character as you get older. In that sense, the pieces always feel new – constant, but constantly surprising. They become part of your private autobiography and every time you conduct them a new layer of memory is added to the bond between you. Each performance is a collection of the experiences you have had together. Not many friendships last so long – I suppose the unchanging nature of the music simplifies the dynamic between you – but what would be an unhealthily one-sided affair in your personal life provides a great deal of comfort throughout your professional one. It is even richer if you can always remember the initial naivety, wonder, and thrill that accompanied your first 'date'.

All conductors have a different set of composers they feel close to at any one time and these affinities are based on a variety of things. A geographical connection can reveal an empathy for a culture you grew up in, or you might just have an instinctive passion for music from a different part of the world. There might be a rapport with a particular period in history or it could be music of your own time that you understand the best. Often the connection is simply a purely personal intuition that defies categorisation.

Whatever the reasons, in all probability the stronger the bond with the composer, the better you conduct the music. Although it can occasionally be problematic if you care too much, the power of your advocacy depends on the sense of personal responsibility you feel. Studying any work begins by trying to identify its composer's ego, and then identifying with that ego yourself. An orchestra responds positively to conductors who have a deep understanding of the composer's identity and who show that serving that identity is the musical purpose of their own.

Some composers make their personalities more readily available than others. Beethoven, Tchaikovsky, or Mahler, for instance, feel very present as individuals within their music. Their ego is a public one that rings out loud and clear. The private lives of Mozart, Brahms, or Ravel, on the other hand, are less relevant to their musical expression, and there are composers whose lives give no clues whatsoever as to what their music means. I have yet to discover anything personal about Bach that got me closer to his compositions. And though I enjoy reading around and about the lives of composers, I wouldn't say it necessarily gives me profounder insights into their music. Performers are not historians and the best music speaks for itself without any need for contextual reference. Researching the circumstances of a composer's life can be invaluable in grasping the voice with which they speak, but it can also be limiting, or even positively unhelpful. It's certainly dangerous to make too great a connection between the lives of composers and their art. Beethoven wrote his happiest symphony just as he discovered he was going deaf. His situation could not be less relevant. Yet the thirteen consecutive exclamation marks that he adds to a line in one particular letter give an indication of the character that defines so much of his musical personality. The fact that Mahler had some therapy sessions with Sigmund Freud might help in appreciating his emotional extremes; to know that he suffered from hae-morrhoids is probably more of a distraction. But Dvořák's Symphony 'From the New World' is clearly a lonely and homesick postcard to the people and country he had left behind; Strauss is confident enough to call his symphonic self-portrait *A Hero's Life*, and Janáček found a vehicle to express the tragic loss of his daughter in *Jenůfa*. Music like this touches us as universal, but it comes with a very strong autobiographical signature.

The greatest composers have a Shakespearean ability to describe things beyond their own experience. The early operas of Mozart are extraordinary not so much for their musical sophistication but for the depth of psychological understanding that no fourteen-year-old can have gained other than through some mysterious inner workings of the soul. Even Shostakovich, whose works are unquestionably the result of the intense suffering of his time, writes music that is far more than a musical chronicle of twentieth-century Russia. Carl Jung believed that, psychologically speaking, we are all constructed the same way. Music taps into these unconscious collective archetypes and turns the personal into something universal while at the same time allowing the universal to feel personal. You realise there is no difference between the two.

★

The emergence of the conducting profession can be at-tributed only in part to a practical solution for dealing with the increasing number of people needed to perform the orchestral music of the nineteenth century. When Haydn reportedly said, on hearing Beethoven's 'Eroica' Symphony, that from then on music would never be the same again, he was presciently acknowledging that most new orchestral music would now be an overtly programmatic experience, and with that was born the idea of a single narrator to tell the 'story' in performance. The composer, no longer the music itself, had become the hero, and the conductor became that hero's advocate. Conductors are, of course, the storytellers not the stories, the ghost writers not the subjects, but the idea of a piece of music having a vivid relationship to the personality, character, and temperament of the composer means that such an emotional narrative can be served well by an individual who is one step removed from the actual playing of it. I don't think it is a coincidence that the 'Eroica' is arguably the first orchestral piece to benefit from constant, albeit extremely subtle, fluctuations of tempo. It is perhaps the first symphony to need a conductor. And I feel the musical and emotional reasons for that are connected. Whether or not composers made the stories behind the notes explicit, the Romantic symphony was a vehicle for personal drama – and one to be interpreted as such, even if only in a subconscious way. Even the generic description of music as 'romantic' suggests a human element rather than a purely musical one. Wagner talked about discovering the 'poetic object' of a piece in order to form an interpretation of it. Music was no longer the end of the expression but the means for it.

Most eighteenth-century music was not intended to be

conducted at all. Either the first violinist of the orchestra or the continuo keyboard player took whatever practical responsibility was necessary. Because it seems as if there is a physical absence of the need for a conductor inherent in the music itself, I always feel rather an intruder when I conduct it – and an emotional impostor as well. The music is about itself, performed originally only by the musicians who are making the sound. Haydn's elegance, for example, comes from an elegance of playing it, and if requested by a third party, such a grace can immediately be made unattainable by its very own self-consciousness. It isn't something that can be manufactured. Similarly, the universal purity of Bach's writing feels somehow compromised the moment it becomes the reflection of a single individual's view.

But by the end of the nineteenth century, a composer such as Mahler saw music as specifically requiring an individual conductor to generate its narrative in performance. Given that often, at least initially, he was that individual, this only exaggerated the sense of music as emotional autobiography. It was not that he wrote highly descriptive music because he was the conductor. Rather he was a conductor because he felt music was too descriptive to be performed without a unified interpretative vision. And there is a physicality in his music that reflects the very conducting of it – his conducting of it in fact. He wrote music to be conducted and the musical language, from its very inception, is integral to the physical language of expressing it. Discovering the right gestures to conduct a composition is much easier when the music itself seems to be the result of the physical gestures of the composer.

Some would argue that imposing a specific programme onto a piece of music limits its breadth of imaginative possibilities. Why do we need stories to define our interpretations? Does not the whole point of music lie in its ability to communicate on a deeper level than words? Abstract music is indeed the ultimate music, the purest that exists – containing meaning only within itself, neither needing explanation nor capable of being described – and despite Haydn's prophecy, there are plenty of abstract orchestral works. A lot of Stravinsky's music, for instance, is totally divorced from a story or extra-musical thread. As are most of the works of Webern and Boulez. In these pieces conductors have to make sure that their own necessarily visible personality does not get in the way of the music's less individual expression. Our very presence can work against the inexplicable profundity of pure music. For if it is the programmatic, rather than the practical, aspect of a piece of music that generates the need for conductors in the first place, it is problematic that, in reverse, a conductor can, simply by being there, suggest a programmatic interpretation even if one is not called for by the piece itself.

*

A classical musician's role is basically a *re*creative one. And recreative artistry is a delicate balancing act. We try to be the medium through which composers speak, but our means of doing that successfully is essentially dependent on our own personality. Performers seek to be invisible, yet know that music cannot be played without us. It's not a straightforward line to tread, either for the individual or for the music business as a whole. Although the personality of the performer is crucial and ultimately what distinguishes great performances, that personality has to be used as a means to an end, an end envisioned fundamentally by the composer.

Non-classical music makes less distinction between composer and performer. Indeed, fans of pop music will often not even know who wrote the song they are hearing. Some classical music lovers do have specific orchestras they like, without minding so much what they play, but most want to listen to a particular piece without worrying about who is performing it. In classical music, the composer is definitely at the top of the tree, and though a few performers generate a fan club, none of them will ever be as famous as Mozart. Nevertheless, musicians expressing music through their own feelings is what keeps it alive and, in that sense, I think pop music's emphasis on the performer is rather healthy.

Music reveals a musician's personality and a musician's personality reveals the music. If musicians aimed only to express themselves, everything they played would sound the same, but if you can mould your own personality to what is suitable for the piece, both composer and performer will be bound together without either sounding restricted. Fortunately, it is not impossible to have a strong ego directed towards expressing someone else's. Oscar Wilde talked about revealing the art but concealing the artist – to be everywhere present but always invisible. There is validity in this paradox.

One of my teachers used to say that 'interpretation' was

something other conductors did. His tongue-in-cheek remark wasn't meant to be arrogant. He was simply saying that conductors should not set out to 'interpret' a piece of music. Our job is to play exactly what composers write, responding to their requests in as genuine a way as possible. Choices have to be made, but whether these choices are spontaneous or predetermined, it is only when they are overly self-conscious that an interpretation loses its sincerity. Stravinsky's complaint that the conducting profession 'rarely attracts original minds' is a surprising one to me. Originality in a conductor seems an odd demand, especially coming from a composer. Of course, one wants to make music sound fresh, but there's an inevitability about genius that should be respected as well. Simply as a goal in itself, originality leads to artificially mannered performances. If the merchandise is perfect, you don't have to sell it.

The music composers write is a gift. It is a gift that invites both contemporary and future generations to discover, explore, and express aspects of who they are as individuals and as a community. It is a link that forms a bridge between the private and the public, the past and the present. It stretches across continents and reaches back through centuries. Music might tell us about our past but it is in the interpretation of it that we discover more about our present. Indeed, a history of the interpretation of classical music is as revealing as the history of music itself. Music is often ahead of its time, yet the interpretation of it is always a reflection of the time of its performance. Composers might often be dead, but at least the performers never are. For me, listening to recordings from the last hundred years provides just as valid a cultural commentary on the twentieth century as the actual music. An Edwardian strictness of tempo gave way to greater flexibility in the 1920s. This led in turn to the cult of the individual, the power of which was curbed by a movement that sought comfort in the composer's authenticity and, philosophically at least, implied that the individual performers themselves were irrelevant. Today our values are less rigid: historically informed, yet not bound by treatises on past performance practices. Interpretations are fashions, changing with the times, and it is this that allows the music to stay relevant. We hear the past through the present, and the present through the past.

*

Over a hundred years have passed since the first recording of a complete symphony was made. In the intervening years almost every professional conductor has committed at least a few of their performances to a permanent medium of some kind or other. Before I knew better, I assumed that these recordings represented the conductor's definitive statement on that particular piece and I viewed this pressure of posterity as a rather inhibiting responsibility. But once I started experiencing the process myself, I realised that achieving a perfect realisation of how I felt the music should sound was an unattainable utopia, and that to attempt to do so actually said more about one's own vanity than one's musical ideals. There might be something to gain from seeking technical perfection, but there are more important things that can be lost as a result along the way.

If you stumble across a piece of music on the radio, you can normally tell immediately whether it's come from a live performance or a studio recording. Some argue that the latter is as far removed from the intended musical experience as a postcard of a work of art is to its original hanging in a gallery. Others say that listening to music within the intimacy of their own private space offers an intense and personal experience that no public venue can replicate. They are obviously completely different artistic experiences and to argue for one or the other is like trying to choose between Haydn and Mozart. The debate is as pointless as it is endless. But there are very few conductors who value the recording wing of the profession more than their public performances and, though this might not have been true thirty years ago, I believe it is live music that currently sustains the recording industry rather than the other way around.

The interesting question to me is whether or not the universal availability of recordings has led to a more homogenous approach to performances around the world. The fact that conductors can easily hear 'how a piece goes' without having to make any decisions about what the composer might have meant does diminish the potential for a genuinely individual response from some, but the most confident musicians are unlikely to have their personalities ironed out by the influence of others. It is true that old distinctions between a Russian, American, French, or Central European conducting tradition are no longer particularly valid but one could just as easily argue that these geographical schools created even more conformity within themselves than the ubiquitous CD does today.

A more dangerous consequence of the power of recordings is that some members of an audience have an expectation that the live performance they hear in the hall will conform to the one they have become accustomed to hearing at home. It's hard not to believe that the way you are used to a piece being performed is the only way you can enjoy it, and who are we, the performers, to deny the right of those who are paying us to have their expectations fulfilled rather than challenged? But even if we wanted to dish up a status quo, we would not be able to do so without knowing which recordings people owned. Conversely, it's a pity if conductors feel a need to be overly idiosyncratic just in order to be noticed. 'I have never heard it played like that before' is a usefully enigmatic post-performance remark. For many it is taken as a compliment. But we shouldn't be disappointed by anyone who thanks us for playing exactly what they wanted to hear. Both are sincere experiences.

Conductors want it both ways. We want audiences to be knowledgeable enough to be conscious of the choices we make and we are stimulated to perform to those who believe they have a right to their own interpretative opinion. But we want them to be thrilled whether we do something they were expecting or not. We want to eat our cake and have it.

★

I feel fortunate to have started conducting after the movement towards greater authenticity rekindled a passion for the precise details of what composers actually wrote, and a curiosity about the musical conventions within which they did so. It is easy to take it for granted now, but it was iconoclastic at the time – a radical revolution that sought originality by looking backwards.

Strictly speaking, the premise of an authentic performance is flawed. Even if you play in the halls or with the instruments for which the music was written, our contemporary points of reference can never be returned to those of the audiences of the past. Today's truth is not yesterday's truth. Our attitude to speed is now related to rockets not horses; our ears have become attuned to an almost limitless degree of amplification, and the world has an ambient soundtrack in which silence has become a surprising quality rather than an underlying one. We cannot unlearn our experience, nor deny our expectation.

Musicians who believe in period practice recognise this, of course. They see their scholarship as a historical means to a contemporary end. They know that listening to music is not like wandering around the glass panels of a museum, and acknowledge that playing it is as much about the performer as it is about the composer. But that doesn't mean that a thorough exploration of what the composer would have expected to hear is irrelevant. Far from it. Knowing this better allows us to find its modern relevance and, in doing so, understand that there's not that much difference between the two.

In the grand scheme of things, Western classical music as we know it is very contemporary. Evolutionarily speaking, human beings haven't changed a jot since Gregorian plainchant gave way to contrapuntal diversity and harmonic complexity. We might have split the atom and discovered anaesthetic, but our attitudes to love and loss, hope and disappointment, remain exactly the same. You need only look to Shakespeare to appreciate how psychologically similar we are to those who lived almost half a millennium before us. The emotions that composers express are understood now just as they were whenever their music was written. Only the way the actual notes are combined has changed. Historically informed performance practice offers a healthy balance between the contexts of past and present and empowers performers to make choices that relate to both. It's a combination that aims to eliminate the time in between. There are only two dates that matter: the date of composition and the date of performance. What is to be avoided is the distance between the two – a sea of habit, a confusion of inherited responses. Authentic interpretation seeks to wipe away the smudgy veneers of tradition that are layered onto a score almost as soon as it is first performed.

Tradition and authenticity should be the same thing, yet in terms of musical performance they quite quickly start to represent polar opposites. They are like twin sisters, separated at birth, creating a confusing dichotomy for both performer and listener as to what the essential truth of a piece is. Normally the word 'tradition' implies something that has always been rather than something subsequently imposed. Yet in music that is patently not the way it is understood. 'Traditional' ways of playing Beethoven and Brahms, for instance, did not arise until the middle of the twentieth century. Widely disseminated by the recording industry, these so-called traditions then became such a part of the music that many people assumed they were the music, and expected to hear them as such. They still do, and there are plenty who say they prefer these 'traditional' interpretations to 'authentic' ones. In fact, the most conservative music lovers are often the hardest to persuade that what they are trying to conserve is not necessarily something the composer actually wanted to hear.

Observing tradition normally means playing things composers did not write. Many of these differences originated because performers, thinking they knew better, or believing they could sound more impressive if they changed something, indulged in choices that said more about themselves than about the music. Some alterations served their vanity, others their limitations. And these bad traditions can stick for the same reasons. I am always glad when violinists choose to play the slow movement of Tchaikovsky's Violin Concerto with a mute as the composer requested, and even happier if they are respectful enough to play its central section at the octave he actually wrote. It doesn't happen very often.

Nevertheless, tradition also has a set of positive values that should not necessarily be disregarded. There are plenty of situations in which, because composers were so connected to the performance practices of their time, they expected to hear something they hadn't written. A tradition can also become established through perfectly valid experiences, and there is nothing wrong with pieces generating a cumulative understanding of how best to play them. After all, we can do better than our predecessors if we start with a knowledge of what they learned themselves. Why would we not want to benefit from the experience of history?

If performers follow traditions mindlessly, they are simply engaging in what Mahler called *Schlamperei* – an untranslatable Austrian word lying somewhere between laziness and sloppiness. But if careful consideration brings you to the same conclusions that many generations have done before, there is a special sense of being part of something bigger. Tradition can serve as a beautiful chain through time, a vibrating string that links both performers and listeners to everyone who has ever played and heard that particular piece. And a tradition arrived at afresh is worth the questioning effort it took to get there. When used, to quote Somerset Maugham, as 'a guide and not a jailer', it allows the performance to sound both spontaneous and inevitable at the same time.

The standard repertoire is so frequently played that our connection to it is in reality diluted by sometimes hundreds of years of other people's ideas. The possibility for generic performances is always there. But players respond to completely new compositions without any such preconceptions. In the absence of a familiar aural tradition, their interpretation can be nothing other than completely genuine. Every time an orchestra plays a well-known work, it does so in relation to its assumptions. Devoid of historical influence, however, musicians have only themselves as the source of expression and the performance is far more personal as a result. Even as exacting and rigorously composed a piece as Boulez's *Rituel*, which I have conducted with a number of orchestras, sounds remarkably different each time. The unbridled sincerity with which musicians approach their parts reinforces exactly how much variety can be lost by repeating so many inherited interpretations.

Most large groups of people are essentially conservative, even if that is not a fair representation of the individuals who make up those groups. An orchestra is no different. For the conductor, it is liberating not to have an orchestra's collective experience of a piece staring you in the face, nor the audience's traditional expectations for it hovering over your shoulder. Both can be a destructive burden. With new music you are free to be the best musician you can be, confident in the knowledge that your interpretation has not been corrupted by anyone else's, and certain that your performance cannot be compared to any that have gone before. You know that people's opinion of the music is going to be more significant than their opinion of the performance – an emphasis that you think you wish was the case more often.

Taken to extremes, both authenticity and tradition represent a recreation of the past that stifles the spontaneous creativity essential to speak to contemporary audiences. Tradition can never be new, and nothing guarantees the death of an art form more than it not being allowed to grow. Compositions are not historical artefacts. Their meaning is constantly being added to. Unlike a painting, a piece of music needs a performance to be brought to life, and in that sense, a composition is never finished. But if addressed with thought and sincerity, authenticity and tradition are a huge part of the decision-making process that conductors go through in our preparation of the score, and play a significant part in developing an understanding of what our response to that score should be. A healthy mix of authenticity, tradition, and spontaneity is better than being a slave to any one of them. It is just as foolish to think that something is good because it is old as it is to think that because something is new it is better.

★

The majority of conductors spend most of their time studying the music they are going to be conducting. It certainly takes up much more of my life than rehearsing or performing. There are as many different ways of preparing a piece as there are conductors but I imagine the motivation to do so is normally the same. You want to know exactly what it is the composer has written so that you can form a firm view of what you believe the piece is expressing. A score is written in code, and though the limitations of this code mean that it can be only the start of your understanding, it's a road map on which everything you think has to be based. Knowledge of the score is the root from which your imagination can grow. Separate the two and the performance will be too much a reflection of the conductor and not enough of the composer. Any fantasy has to be based on the reality of the score.

This reality is not as precise as one might wish. Irrespective of the particular published edition you use, a printed score is always in some way an interpretation of the autograph manuscript the composer leaves behind. The scholarship that goes into producing an *Urtext* is invaluable but the decisions that inevitably need to be made to turn the composer's handwriting into something of practical use are still editorial. Only by studying a facsimile of an original manuscript yourself can you be sure that you are looking at exactly what the composer wrote. I wouldn't say that any of my performances have been improved by anything specific I have discovered for myself but in many cases the emotion that seeps out from behind the handwriting is incredibly affecting. Composers such as Mozart and Strauss wrote out their scores so perfectly that there is a disconcerting sense of clinical detachment, one that provides few clues as to how the music should be played. The handwriting of Beethoven and Janáček on the other hand reveals all the struggle and torment that went into their compositional process. You can see which bars mattered to them the most, and which ones they considered to be relatively by the by. Sometimes these clues can make a big difference to the musical decisions you make. At other times it just feels special to be close to the source of the music on a human level. To look at the ever-diminishing content in the manuscript of Mahler's last symphony is to feel as if you are watching a man die before your very eyes. It is intensely moving, even without hearing the actual music.

Despite the extra connection a manuscript affords, however, it is not necessarily the best use of a performer's time to spend hours and hours poring over a Beethovenian scribble to determine whether a dot or a dash is in fact a dash and a dot. On the whole scholars and performers have a different set of skills and their roles are probably best kept apart. The best editors see scholarship as enabling the composer's musical truth to be heard in performance. The best performers know that that truth is unlikely be found without this scholarship in the first place.

Good published editions allow you to get closer to what the composers wrote, but knowing what they mean is always going to be a combination of musical experience and emotional intuition. Although a composer can prescribe a huge range of expressive nuances, the exact purpose of any of them is indeterminate. In the early days of orchestral music, performers were lucky if they got any at all. This was certainly not because the music itself needed less subtlety in its performance, and the composer's likely involvement in the rehearsals would have prevented the absence of written details resulting in anything bland. But I think the lack of detail in early scores is more an indication of the perceived limits of their value to define musical expression.

Understanding the contemporary conventions of the time goes a long way in helping you to decide if the composers are writing in a sort of musical shorthand that they expected performers to be familiar with, or whether they are wanting you to take a more literal approach. A great deal of early orchestral music, for instance, evolved out of long-established dance forms. The tempos and rhythms of a gavotte or a gigue would have been ingrained in the players' bones. Nor would note lengths and dynamics have merited much discussion within a musical culture that was naturally understood. Composers had better things to do than to detail what they knew their performers knew too and it's unlikely there were many who realised they were writing for posterity as well. Once that changed, composers became more specific in their instructions, but still the most precise notation is powerless in the face of the almost limitless subtleties of musical imagination.

We live in a society in which many are comfortable trading truth as much as any other commodity, but in cultural spheres at least great value is still placed on staying faithful to the original text of the composer. It was not always so. In the past, broad consciences thought they could best serve the music by updating it to 'benefit' from, for instance, developments made to a newer instrument's greater range of pitch or volume. The argument was that we should make the most of modern progress and embrace possibilities that did not exist at the time a piece was being written. Bigger was always considered better. Larger halls needed louder orchestras. Louder orchestras made conductors feel more important.

The idea of changing what is written cannot just be dismissed as dilettantish however. Pierre Boulez once told me that he felt the fixed nature of printed texts can run contrary to constantly evolving conceptions on the part of composers: what they wrote on one day was not necessarily what they wanted to hear on another. But though altering an orchestration can help bring out a salient line, or enable a better balance to be achieved with less effort, it seems to me that once crossed, this line is a hard one to navigate beyond. Mahler said that conductors should feel free to change anything that they did not think sounded right, though I suspect he was advocating more on behalf of Mahler the conductor than Mahler the composer. The majority of performers nowadays feel it is more sincere to work within the confines of what the composer wrote and only what would have been possible at the time. The sound world of every composer is intrinsically linked to the instrumental capabilities of their day and working outside that original framework distorts that sound's perspective, diminishing rather than extending the power of the piece. Performers need to inhabit every piece they play, but a sense of ownership should fall short of knocking down walls and rearranging the furniture. It might well be that composers would have wanted to make the most of the more elaborate orchestral toybox we have at our disposal today, but this is a hypothetical scenario and music is hypothetical enough without adding any more guesswork into the mix. Anyway, there is nothing more paralysing to the imagination than endless possibilities. Freedom can be very complicated.

Most of the time we should remain within the instrumental framework that each composer imagined but we cannot deny progress when it comes to the abilities of orchestra players. No one knows what standards were like before the advent of recording. Although anecdotal evidence suggests, for instance, that the musicians of the Vienna Philharmonic thought Schubert's 'Great' C major Symphony was technically absurd, I wonder if there has been as much improvement as we like to imagine. Composers extend the boundaries of what is playable, yet only in exceptional circumstances do they overreach them completely. Most push at the walls of limitation from within. Still, today's orchestras can play pretty much anything that is put in front of them and we can rarely replace the sense of human effort that must have gone into performing scores that were originally considered impossible. Even the most difficult music can now be played to a certain standard with minimal rehearsal. This is not necessarily an advantage. Mozart wrote that he wanted the finale of his 'Haffner' Symphony to be played 'as fast as possible'. Did he mean as fast as orchestras of his day could play or as fast as any orchestra could ever play? Was it an extreme he was after for its own sake or did he imagine something more specific? Take the stress out of performances and, in some cases, something very fundamental to the piece is lost as well. Nowadays the challenge of performing Stravinsky's *The Rite of Spring* is to make sure it still sounds difficult. The intensity of the musical challenges of the past are hard to replicate through the contemporary lens of an inverted telescope.

★

The first time you look at a score, it is rather like reading a novel. Your initial curiosity is to find out whether it has a happy ending or not. Looking at it again, you start to appreciate more subplots within the narrative, and how these relate to the story as a whole. Slowly you begin to pick up more of the characterisation. You start to hear adjectives within the melodies, feel the adverbs of the rhythm and, each time you go through it, extra layers are revealed. The more you hear in the score, the more the audience will hear too, and the better you know the piece, the easier it is to imagine its meaning. The security that comes from understanding this meaning makes it much easier to be free to express it. You study the score over and over again, and then you study it more. You keep studying it until the time comes when you know that you need the musicians themselves to take the score to a deeper level. For there is a limit to the number of questions that can be answered without the reality of sound and tempo that comes from the orchestra and its live playing of the piece. At its most interesting, studying a score is studying a series of choices, and you know the ramifications of those choices only once you hear how an orchestra plays them.

You want to arrive at the first rehearsal with a set of options, credible enough for a genuine choice rather than a dilemma, and you need the ability to choose between these possibilities and take ownership of the consequences of those choices as quickly as possible. It's easier to do this if they come from a place of freedom, not doubt. There is time for one, not the other. Of course, you have to know a piece well enough to be able to hear whether there are any wrong notes being played in the rehearsal, and if so exactly what they are and who is playing them, but this musical proofreading ability becomes important only if there *are* mistakes. It is a crucial skill, but not an achievement in itself. Orchestras are glad when the conductor hears an error that they themselves hadn't noticed. But this is the minimum they expect. Indeed a 'correct' performance can be quite a damning criticism. Studying a score is not about learning *what* the music is, but trying to understand what the music *is*.

Hearing the score as you read it is the most direct connection you can have with the composer. Without the orchestra musicians, or your conducting of them, the one-to-one communication can be intensely rewarding. This imaginative privacy offers a profound, albeit self-centred, engagement with who you really are and which aspects of the music touch you the most. But music was written to be an audible, not a virtual, reality. Orchestral music – unlike chamber music, for instance – can never be a private passion. A solitary approach limits both the music and your own enjoyment of it. Music is about life and it needs people to keep it alive.

Depending on your own musical proficiency, some scores are hard to hear just by looking at them. Schoenberg's *Moses und Aron*, for instance, doesn't mean much to me in isolation. The piano can be a guide to figuring out exactly what certain chords and melodies are going to sound like but you need to be a very brilliant pianist to reveal the full range of a composer's orchestral palette. If taking care of musical colour and line are two of the most important responsibilities for a conductor, the piano is not necessarily the best tool with which to explore them. Only in the finest fingers can the black-and-white nature of the keyboard translate into an orchestra's vast range of instrumental sonority, and a piano's percussive nature makes it hard to look after what happens to the sound once the note has been played. That is exactly what great pianists do, but if you are that good, it seems rather a waste not to be playing the piano all the time. As an aid, the piano can be extremely useful, but I am certainly aware of the point at which my pianistic facility, or lack thereof, starts to limit musical creativity.

Most conductors admit to listening to recordings as a valuable way to deepen their understanding of a piece. How could you not have something to learn from others who in all probability have performed the work in question many times before they feel it is appropriate to record their opinions, passions, and experience of it onto a disc for posterity? It can be extremely beneficial to hear things that confirm your own opinions and it can be equally instructive, perhaps even more so, to listen to performances that you feel do not work. To be aware of the possibility of what you perceive to be wrong choices helps you to avoid them yourself. Other conductors' interpretations can provoke you to change your mind, but they can also strengthen your conviction and it isn't difficult to admire someone else's performance while holding on to the integrity of your own.

The danger of listening to recordings is not that you listen to too many but that you listen to too few. The greater the piece, the more opinions about it vary. Depending on your own level of confidence, the diversity of interpretations of Beethoven's music, for instance, is either liberating or daunting. Performances of pieces by composers such as Cherubini or Spohr, however, sound remarkably alike. Variety of interpretation is clearly a good thing, and only in a limited piece are there limitations in performance. But being confused by how many possibilities there are is more easily resolved than the difficulty of coming under the spell of just one. This is when the influence of a particular recording robs you of your own artistic identity. If you can wait to listen to recordings until the middle or end of your preparation process, you can first discover your own individual response to the piece, and a bedrock of belief is established that can then factor in more healthily the valuable experience of others.

The uniqueness of every great performance derives large-ly from the artistic honesty of the performer. When per-formers are sincere, their performances are as unique as they are. In contrast, disengaging your true self from the performance is disingenuous: either you make a musically generic choice, or you copy someone else and end up with a self-conscious imitation. A second-hand musical idea can never carry the same weight as the authority of your own. Dostoevsky wrote that it was better to tell your own lies than someone else's truth: 'In the first case you are a man, in the second no more than a parrot.'

It is tempting to assume that recordings made by the com-posers themselves are especially valuable. In an obvious sense they are, but even if the composers in question are good con-ductors there are plenty of reasons why what they recorded might not be a valid reflection of what they want other con-ductors to do. Composers engage in music creatively, and when they conduct, that genuine creativity remains. This is clear when you listen to their own recordings and hear where they contradict what they have written. It creates a dilemma as to which is the more reliable source. Should we perform what composers write or what they play?

In Rachmaninov's case for instance, the difference is sig-nificant. He was a wonderful conductor and a great pianist. His performance legacy cannot be dismissed, and those who argue that his practical experience as a performer should override his achievements as a composer have a fair point. My view, however, is that the score should remain the authority. I have made enough CDs to appreciate that final versions do not always represent exactly what I had envisioned, and in the early days of recording there must have been several variables that prevented composers feeling they had created definitive performances, or even that that is how those recordings would be perceived.

Elgar's recordings might be victims of circumstance too. Fabulous documents though they are – one can almost hear the twirling of Edwardian moustaches – not many would uphold his choice of tempi as being preferable to those he wrote. Some composer–conductors in the past lacked the physical technique to achieve their wishes. When a timorous record producer remarked to Stravinsky that his second take was faster than the first, the composer said he liked the second version better. This retort was possibly a smokescreen for his conducting failings, but we cannot be sure. How do we know if something we hear is the result of a composer's weakness as a performer or a confession that the composer-as-performer's subsequent ideas are preferable? Such uncertainty is what keeps pieces alive. Plenty might disagree with the solutions performers opt for, but few dispute the performer's right to make those choices.

I cannot remember which pope said that 'to get to the source of a river, you have to row upstream'. For all musicians, studying a score is hard work, and for conductors the internal nature of how we prepare makes it feel like an especially solitary demand. 'The Loneliness of the Long-Distance Conductor' indeed. Singing the parts while you are learning them can help create a more active link between you and the music but it doesn't offer the same connection that is available to practising instrumentalists. What increases the vulnerability of the process is that you are very rarely taught how to do it. Conducting lessons tend to focus on the physicality and – one hopes – the musicianship required, but how to approach a score, what to look for, and why, is often neglected. Perhaps there is a feeling that it is considered too individual a process. But it is for that very reason that guidance can be extremely helpful. My teacher would remark that although conducting couldn't be taught, there were still plenty of aspects to it that could be learned. That's true – but then there is even more reason to be taught how to learn.

Conducting students are encouraged to go to as many professional rehearsals as possible. I went often, loved doing so, and felt privileged to be able to get to know the music in its 'backstage' form. But I'm not convinced I learned that much. In fact, I would often go home feeling extremely puzzled by what I had just seen, and over time I realised that the greater the conductor, the more confused I was. Even the players I talked to would disagree about the specifics involved and, despite an occasional unanimity of admiration, there was never a consensus on why this was the case.

The journey away from being a student is the journey towards finding out what you have to offer as an individual, discovering what you feel about the music, and working out how best to align your own physiology to express it. The problem with trying to learn from watching great conductors is that one of the things that makes them great is that they are unique. I cannot think of any two, dead or alive, who are similar either musically, physically, or psychologically, and the moment students start to copy one is the moment they identify themselves as students. It is perhaps more useful to watch those who show you what *not* to do, and you would probably learn more by attending bad rehearsals. But that was hard to believe as a starstruck young wannabe.

★

The best performances reveal a score's details without losing perspective on the overarching narrative of the piece. It is easy to mistake the wood for the trees but as long as the details serve the whole, it is possible to value both. In more complicated pieces you can get bogged down by all the instructions the composer gives you. If you don't dot an 'i' or cross a 't', they can both look like an 'l', but, despite its value, due diligence mustn't sound like a goal in itself. Pedantry can take you further away from the music rather than closer to it, and you can soon discover you are playing the information rather than using it. Although some people might be more interested in a lecture on heaven than heaven itself, I hope they are in the minority. Musical details are a means of expression rather than the expression itself. You have to think meaning not grammar – be like a chef who doesn't want you to be able to taste any of the ingredients.

The inspiring French pedagogue Nadia Boulanger said that 'to study music, we must learn the rules. To create music, we must break them . . . A great work is made out of a combination of obedience and liberty.' She was talking more about composing but the philosophy of performing is similar. Great musicians are ruled not by the score but by their passion for it, a compulsion that is much easier to follow within the context of a live performance. This is not wilful individualism but a belief that music is a life-giving force that gets its oxygen from the ardency that feeds it. The discipline of the mind provides structure for the piece but it is the enthusiasm of the heart that creates the generosity of spirit audiences want to be part of. When Stravinsky said that it was more important to love a piece than to respect it, he was describing his view of the relationship between performers and composers. Love implies respect as well, but his point is that the connection should be more an emotional than an intellectual one. Most of the time we need a reverential humility in the face of works of art that are far more significant than we could ever be, but at the moment of the performance we are part of that work of art and must have a subjective attachment to it if we are to do it justice. Respect keeps its distance. Love gets involved. There is no denying which is more powerful.

It is said that wisdom is understanding how and when to use your knowledge. Excessive preparation is a waste of time if your knowledge simply functions as a cage that stifles spontaneity rather than as a climbing frame for creativity. Some believe that only in spontaneity can truth be found. I certainly think that musical instinct is just as powerful as knowledge – and even more so in the most intuitive musicians. A natural conviction is more infectious than a studied one, and it persuades with a lightness of touch that is far more successful than a heavy-handed one.

*

In most Western classical music, compositions have a beginning, a middle, and an end. With certain minimalist exceptions, if you drop into a piece at any random point you will have a rough idea where you are. This is not the case with the majority of pop songs, which are generally three-minute snapshots of one particular mood. The greater attention span required by classical music is rewarded by the performer's consciousness of a need to pace the journey inherent within the piece. With large-scale orchestral works, steering this voyage is something I believe only the conductor can do.

In the human brain the areas that respond to musical emotion and to musical structure are not in the same place. How they relate to each other presumably affects the sort of music we enjoy. It also explains why conductors vary in how much they prioritise form over content. Some think that by concentrating on getting the level of emotion right the big picture will take care of itself. I feel that you need a bird's-eye view before you can control how emotional each moment should be. It's rather like being a tour guide. You encourage people to stop and look at a sight, but perhaps not for long because there is a better one around the corner. You lead the listener up and down, round and about, but always with the destination in mind. There can only be one climax in a work, and pacing its arrival and controlling its catharsis can take patience and self-discipline. Every event must be proportional to the whole. Performers need a conscious understanding of where the piece is loudest and where it is quietest; which section is the most active, and which the most passive; where is its peak and where is its trough. For me a good performance is a series of comparatives structured around a single superlative.

The structure of a piece of music is like the structure of a novel. A book can be split into parts, chapters, paragraphs, sentences, and words. Each of these words has a syllable that is stressed, each sentence a contour, each paragraph a purpose, each chapter an identity, and all relate to the narrative overall. A musical composition is formed by a similar series of levels, each of which shapes the one immediately above it. The accent of each motive defines the outline of a phrase. The phrase fashions the musical paragraph it belongs to and the paragraphs mould the design of the entire movement. Understanding the hierarchy of these relationships allows you to create the architecture of the piece, an architecture that more often than not is based on the natural beauty and power of the golden ratio.

The Greek concept of a fundamentally satisfying geometric proportion that is as relevant to art as it is to nature underpins the design of much Western classical music. There is a point on a fixed length at which the relationship between the shorter section and the longer one is the same as between the longer one and the whole. Of course, it is stretching the argument to say that the emotional highpoint of every piece of music is just shy of two-thirds of the way through, but it is surprising how often it is valid, for both small- and large-scale musical structures. The apex of most four-bar phrases is somewhere around the third bar. The most significant point of sonata form is when the opening music returns about two-thirds of the way through. The opening six-bar melody of Wagner's music-drama *Parsifal* peaks at exactly this point, just as the most intense moment of the whole piece occurs right before the end of the second of its three acts. A consciousness of this essential ratio allows a conductor to pace the emotional journey of the performance to reflect it. It is a vital part of the storyteller's role.

Until I learn them well, most pieces of music seem quite long to me. But, like all journeys, they start to feel shorter the better I understand the route they take. Knowing where you are going is key to bringing people with you, and envisioning the climax of a work as you embark on its opening helps focus the sense of its destination. For though the pinnacle of the piece may fall towards its end, the magnetic power of that climax needs to be a constant presence within your overall conception. Having the confidence to linger but never stop, to take time but never wait, to speed up but not overshoot, comes from developing and then trusting your appreciation of the music's design.

Storytelling is about managing a journey to a denouement that feels unanticipated, yet, with hindsight, is inevitable too. However unexpected, artistic truth needs to be instantly believable, and you prepare the ground for credible surprise by making sure that every step along the way feels logical yet spontaneous – a balance of predetermination and free will. You need to remember where you have been, be conscious of where you are, and remain certain of where you are going. T. S. Eliot could easily have been discussing music when he wrote in his *Four Quartets*: 'Time present and time past/Are both perhaps present in time future,/And time future contained in time past.'

★

The most obvious role of the conductor is indeed the most basic one. Choosing a speed and communicating that choice to the musicians and then maintaining it strictly or varying it with flexibility is a part of the job that unites us all, whatever our musical circumstances. It is as relevant a skill for the conductor of a primary-school recorder group as it is for the music directors of the richest orchestras in the world.

Getting the tempo right creates an environment in which everything falls effortlessly into place. Seeking this truth is the heart of the musical challenge and finding it lies at the centre of almost every solution to any difficulty. In my experience, if something doesn't sound right, more often than not it is the choice of tempo that is to blame. The music is either too fast to breathe or too slow to feel alive; rhythms cannot find their character unless there is a pulse enabling that discovery to happen; and an ideal speed allows players to hop on and off the musical 'train' without anything sounding dislodged.

Usually the speed that's right for the music is right for the musicians too. Players can therefore normally tell whether the conductor has got it right or not. An ease of playing is synonymous with a musical ease and a listening conductor should be able to hear the result of a physically awkward tempo. That's not to say that the right tempo is the easiest tempo. Ease is not the same as easy. But there is a difference between difficult and impossible, and if we overstep that line, either by wanting the music to be too slow to sustain or too fast to be heard, we will run into problems sooner or later. Forcing an orchestra into a tempo is usually a mistake. If the players are resistant, and this is a musical resistance not a personal one, there is probably a very valid reason behind it. And it is an unequal battle. Not because there are a hundred of them and one of us but because they are likely to have the composer on their side as well.

An orchestra musician once told me that playing a piece at the wrong tempo was like being forced to listen to a recording you didn't like when you knew there was a better one next to it on your shelf. It can be deeply frustrating, as well as difficult, to have to express yourself within a speed you do not agree with. A job in an orchestra has always come with these restrictions, but finding the right tempo is one of the best ways a conductor can avoid a sense of *dis*-ease within the orchestra. We experience this ourselves when a concerto soloist insists on a tempo that we don't believe in. Our professional charge is to do what the soloist wants but it can still feel as if our ability to be convincing is compromised. This is what orchestra players have to do an enormous amount of the time, and they have to find the advantages of such compromises. For conductors, however, to be able to hear music at the speed we think it should go is one the most substantial privileges of the profession.

The traditional way that composers instruct performers as to the appropriate tempo for their music is a set of the most beautifully understated commands imaginable. The word *andante* derives from the Italian simply meaning 'to go'. *Allegro* is perhaps most literally translated as 'cheerful'. The vagueness of these terms is all-encompassing and their eloquent simplicity reveals a fabulous amount of trust from the composer. Or at least an acknowledgement that if performers do not feel the right mood with minimal guidance, a more detailed description is not going to help. Apart from the tempo indications that are intentionally connected to traditional dance forms – and knowing what those dances are is an enormous help to understanding the speeds they demand – most are descriptions of atmosphere rather than of speed, a recognition that speed is in fact always relative. What is slow for a hare is not slow for a tortoise. Such relativity applies to the identity of the composer as well. The music critic Neville Cardus made the fascinating observation that 'every composer has his own basic tempo which decrees that speed in his music is not the same as speed in any other composer'. His point is that you cannot cross-reference a Beethoven *allegro* with one by Schubert. Character on the other hand is far more specific. 'Lively' has a relevance for everyone whatever their resting pulse. At school we learn that *adagio* means slow but actually it means 'at ease'. It is the feeling of the music that controls the tempo. Not the other way round. Only in a marching band does the tempo come first.

Understand the character and the speed will follow. And choosing tempi on that basis allows for a far greater flexibility when it comes to adapting tempi to fit a wide range of differing acoustics. Every hall requires an adjustment in order to create what sounds right in that particular space. The longer the reverberation, the slower the music has to be. A performance of a Bruckner symphony in St Paul's Cathedral will last a lot longer than one in a multi-purpose convention centre. But adapting tempi doesn't mean ceasing to remain true to the composer's vision of what you are trying to recreate. It simply recognises that sound is a physical thing with waves that have properties beyond your control.

An orchestra's technical accomplishment also affects the choice of tempo. Some orchestras can play the Overture to Mozart's *The Marriage of Figaro* with such dexterity and finesse that a fast tempo sounds like a glass of champagne. Less good orchestras might make the same tempo sound like six glasses of champagne. A conductor has to listen to what it actually sounds like. An orchestra that rushes will make the speed sound too fast and an orchestra that drags will make your interpretation feel too slow. An intention based on a very valid opinion made in the vacuum of your own study has to be connected to the reality of what it sounds like. It is what you hear, not what you want to hear, that determines whether your choice is right or not.

How you interpret what you hear is, however, affected by the biggest variable of all: your own ever-fluctuating heartbeat. Perception of speed is related to the pulse of the person hearing it. The stereotypical reason that young conductors often conduct faster than old conductors is simply that their heart is beating faster. The stress of doing something for the first time creates an adrenalin rush that distorts your sense of time. What seems fast to you can easily feel too fast to everyone else. But audiences are not nervous; nor are they engaging in an aerobic workout. And it's their experience that counts. They are the ones who have paid for their tickets. When I was younger, I was sometimes horrified to hear back the recording of a concert I had done. What had felt exciting to me the night before just sounded frenetic the morning after, even with an allowance for the fact that our attitude to pulse is influenced by the time of day. In the right context breathlessness can be thrilling. Hyperventilation, less so. Over time, experience affords you a more rational heartbeat during performances and you learn to make allowances for its implications when judging the appropriateness of your choices of tempo.

Some conductors take great pride in all their performances of any one particular piece taking exactly the same length of time. They feel this shows they have a rock-solid musical conviction. Others take a more liquid view and embrace the potential for their interpretations to vary from night to night. There's validity in both approaches and no reason why you have to stick to just one or the other. But how long the performance lasts is not the same as how long it feels. People listen to music in part to escape the tyranny of the clock of life, subjugating the tick-tock of reality to the illusion of something less mundane. Good performances feel short. The best feel timeless.

*

When Johann Maelzel, the rather eccentric inventor, and occasional friend of Beethoven, created a machine that allowed composers to define every musical tempo, the hope must have been that a performer would never again misunderstand a composer's intentions when it came to speed. But the fact that time and the perception of time can differ to such an extent means that the metronome is a problematic aid. Music is an ever-changing flow of sound for which the word 'metronomic' is often used derogatively. Although defining the number of beats per minute is a straightforward way of establishing the most basic pulse of a piece, and as a guide can be incredibly helpful, music is not a science. Most composers would prefer you to take the time and trouble to understand the speed of a work from within. According to Brahms, 'The metronome is of no value. I have never believed that my blood and a mechanical instrument go well together.'

Composers, and conductors too for that matter, tend to hear music on the fast side. The better you know a piece, the faster your brain can process hearing it. When you 'listen' internally to the music, it is easy to divorce yourself from the physical reality of its sound. With Beethoven, his deafness might have exacerbated this discrepancy. That is not to say his metronome markings are wrong, but giving them a margin in which to breathe can make all the difference to a large audience listening to a large orchestra in a large hall. And even Beethoven himself, who was in on the invention of the metronome at the start, was the first to admit that it had a limited function: 'Feeling also has its tempo.'

This 'feeling' is, of course, constantly changing and what might be an appropriate mood for the start of a piece can become less relevant later on in the music. Equally, a metronome mark can refer to the broad conception of a movement and not necessarily to its opening bars. Although it is misguided to think that Baroque and Classical music should always be played with a strict and uninterrupted pulse, it is true to say that it's the music of the Romantic era that requires a constant fluctuation of tempo to express the freedom of its personality. The emotional journey of a nineteenth-century work is navigated mainly by an ever-changing speed of travel, and a conductor's ability to understand and control *rubato* is key to moulding the structure and style of a performance. For Wagner, 'tempo is the soul of music', and in all music, not just his own, he believed it should be perpetually modified. Music's character, or the *melos* as he called it, was ever-changing, and the tempo should therefore be continually adjusted to reflect that.

Composers differ in how often they prescribe changes of tempo or how much they trust the conductor to influence the pulse more instinctively. The danger of dictating too much variability is that in unsympathetic hands such instructions can sound disjointed. The problem with not enough guidance is that unless the conductor feels empowered to express the flexibility of the music it can feel static and one-dimensional. Given how free Wagner's music needs to be and how egocentric the man was, it is surprising that he prescribed so little. But he knew that words could be easily misunderstood and believed that if conductors are not intuitive enough to feel the *rubato* themselves, they are never going to be able to create it in others, however much extra-musical help they are given.

Mahler, on the other hand, more celebrated in his lifetime as a conductor than a composer, was able to use his practical experience to write brilliantly perceptive instructions to help other conductors steer the ever-changing activity of his music. His use of language is sometimes lightly nuanced, sometimes not. He asks for 'imperceptible' changes of speed, and we know from his letters that he was thrilled to have discovered the subtle power of the negative command. 'Don't drag!' was his way of making the music go faster without a definite sense of *accelerando*. 'Don't rush!' slows it down without a feeling that brakes have been applied. I love the psychology at work here. Asking for the tempo to be 'not too quick' is a polite way of making sure performers play slightly more slowly than they might imagine. And requesting that the music be 'not too slow' avoids any possibility of self-indulgence. Mahler's elusive alterations need more care than his bipolar swings of mood but in each case it is the motivation behind the changes that determines whether they can be achieved successfully. Knowing when the music should speed up or slow down is one thing, but understanding why it needs to is far more important. A *rallentando* is not the same as a *ritenuto*. The first slows the tempo through relaxation, the second because of a heightened intensity. They have the same result, but for completely different reasons. Some increases in speed need to sound as if you are pressing on the accelerator, others should feel as if you have simply released your foot off the brake. Puccini used eleven different phrases to slow the music down in *La bohème*. On a metronome they sound similar, but the emotional differences could not be more varied.

Classical music is a voyage made possible by a series of thwarted expectations. Composers control the trip through dissonance and consonance, and the time taken between the two, but managing the precise nature of that time is mostly the responsibility of the performer. Controlling tension is the fundamental way of influencing a narrative. This is not a question of playing in time or out of time. It is about using time. It takes discipline and freedom, and knowing which to instil at every given moment. Even the most sentimental music needs to be protected from sounding indulgent, whereas liberty should always be rooted within an underlying sense of purpose and direction. The dog that stops at every lamp post takes a long time to get to the end of the street. Unless the composer clearly wants a sudden and noticeable change of direction, *rubato* should always sound effortless. Gear changes should rarely be heard, and for that to be the case it's best if you can always be one step ahead of the next shift. A good driver will know what speed the car needs to be doing to manoeuvre round the next bend smoothly, and looking ahead puts you in the best position to effect any change. Conducting is no different. It is always the future that leads the present.

*

When it comes to dynamics, the composer's ability to be precise is even more constrained than the language available to define its speed. What does 'loud' mean anyway? Baby crying loud or pneumatic drill loud? Should 'quiet' imply a whisper or a summer breeze? The earliest surviving Western classical music specifies no dynamics. Baroque music often made do with a simple loud or soft instruction and with each subsequent generation the level of prescribed detail increased. Over time a basic spectrum of volumes emerged, from triple *piano* at one end to triple *forte* at the other. Notwithstanding extreme cases, such as Tchaikovsky, who wrote *pppppp* in his 'Pathétique' Symphony, or Mahler's use of *fffff* in his Seventh, the volume of most music is crudely divided into only about eight separate categories. Yet human hearing can differentiate between around 120 degrees of volume, a sensitivity that deserves to be rewarded by a similar dynamic sophistication on the part of the performers.

To my knowledge no one has yet come up with the idea of a decibel counter that could do for dynamics what the metronome attempts to do for speed. Perhaps even more than is the case with tempo, when it comes to volume there is a recognition that, divorced from context, too detailed a differentiation is pointless. A single *forte* marking in a work that includes passages with four of them might not be as loud as an occasion in which it is the loudest dynamic of the piece. Interpreting dynamics has a lot to do with style. As instruments have evolved, and musical passion become more explicit, so too has our interpretation of dynamics developed. A trombone section is not going to play a *fortissimo* passage in a Schubert symphony at the same level as it would in one by Mahler. Composers also vary between those who mark the dynamic they want a player to play and those who mean it to refer to the volume they want the audience to hear. *Forte* on a low note on a flute sounds about the same as *piano* on a tuba. *Forte* does not mean 'loud' anyway; it means 'strong'. Depending on the circumstances, that can be expressed in a wide range of volumes. Considered in isolation any particular volume is relatively meaningless.

The word 'dynamic' implies emotional character just as much as musical volume. Seeing volume as a result of character and not the other way round allows for an expressive rather than abstract context to the sound. Whether a *forte* is angry or boisterous is part of the interpretation. Should a *piano* passage be intense or calm? There is a big difference between feeling sad and feeling miserable. A conductor needs to be confident about the sort of the sound the dynamics imply. Although the volume might be the same, the purpose of that volume is multifaceted. *Pianissimo* is a quality not a decibel. To call for more nobility in a phrase or to ask for an atmosphere of intimacy in a solo is far more relevant than trying to dictate exactly how loud it should actually be.

The idea that there are only a few specific volumes is clearly absurd. Musicians are constantly enriching their part's simplistic notation themselves, but, in an orchestral context, precise leadership for controlling such elaboration falls primarily to the conductor. A conductor-less orchestra is perfectly capable of choosing the right tempo, and with plenty of rehearsal time can establish a totally convincing flexibility of pulse. But in terms of sound it is hard for individual musicians to tell exactly how they balance within the group. Despite the mores of our time, music maintains the view that some ideas are more deserving of attention than others and a hierarchy of colour, sonority, and volume can be well judged by a conductor's central, slightly elevated position.

From where we stand we can hear the orchestra as a single sound, and balance the parts to create either a homogeneity of colour or a variety of textures. Like a producer in front of a recording console, we are constantly adjusting the levels of each voice to make our own view of the sonic hierarchy of the piece audible to the audience. If the players know which instrument the audience should be listening to, they will make adjustments themselves. In a well-known piece they do this subconsciously. If the whole orchestra is marked *piano*, the most important line will play a little more and the others less. Players don't need a conductor for this to happen. But how much more or less can make a big difference, especially in less familiar works. Musicians work within very small degrees of separation, and the clarity of a conductor's hearing can create a subtlety of balance that is endlessly shifting and constantly revealing. In a well-balanced orchestra you will be able to hear every part as part of a whole, a sound that is as interesting for its inner detail as it is for the unity of its overview.

The conductor is also the individual who can best encourage a large group of people to push at the boundaries of dynamic range. And though extreme loudness is relatively easy to encourage, the quietest sounds are much harder for orchestras to achieve. As far as the musicians are concerned, exceptionally soft playing can be rewarding if they sense a positive purpose behind it, but it will not be successful if it is repressive and imposed purely for effect. There should never be any denial in music-making. Yet a whisper is often more riveting than a scream, and the extra attention from the audience demanded by a magical hush generates a level of intensity beyond the purely musical. Forcing people to engage in the all but inaudible brings them closer – almost literally. The audience becomes active rather than passive, and takes a more significant role in the community of expression.

Every nuance the composer asks for needs to be turned into some kind of musical narrative. Accents, colours, or any marking beyond the notes themselves, are tools that help musicians tell the story. The range of possibilities is far more than the limited number of hieroglyphic signs that musical notation provides. The word *crescendo* means the music gets louder, but not whether it should do so through generosity or determination, suggestion or encouragement. Musical symbols are a means and not an end, and precise musical expression can be more rewardingly achieved if there is a clarity of emotional thought behind it. And musical expression does need to be exact. We credit ourselves with living in an emotional age, yet we are a generation that can hide the complexity of our true feelings behind the effortless click of a simple emoji. Music must avoid the bland and call out the insincere.

Emotional communication from the conductor is hard for an orchestra to ignore. It is difficult for a musician to sound *dolce cantabile* if the conductor looks *appassionato agitato*. Players can relatively effortlessly choose to bypass a tempo that a conductor tries to set; to a certain extent they can listen to each other to maintain their own view of how much *rubato* the music should have, and they can play more loudly or softly than a conductor's gestures without any problem whatsoever. But if an emotional sense of sonority, the pressure within the sound and the intensity of its delivery, is deeply felt by the conductor, a natural physical communication of it is not easy to disregard.

*

A strong grasp of musical architecture, an appropriate judgement of tempo, and a sensitivity towards colour and balance are relatively straightforward to share with an orchestra. But a far more subtle, almost subconscious, communication is required when it comes to the more delicate nuances of taste. In a musical context these terms are not readily defined. And they change from one generation to the next. Taste is where an individual and society meet, and at the very highest level of music-making, where technical ability and expressive power are a given, it is taste that defines you as a conductor. With it you can explore contrasts without contradiction, and unify expression without limitation. You can reflect Mozart's romanticism through an eighteenth-century sensibility, honour Beethoven's intimacy as much as his rhetoric, prevent Rachmaninov's sentiments from sounding sentimental, and give equal weight to Elgar's Edwardian elegance and his Victorian pride.

Every society has its own consensus of what constitutes good taste and with this comes a danger of it being used by performers as a protective substitute for more personal feelings. This is probably one of the reasons it comes in for such disdain. 'The last resort of the second-rate mind' was Schoenberg's opinion, while Picasso considered it an 'enemy of creativity'. Brecht felt it 'more important to be human'. Such vilification arises from the potential of good taste to be insincere. But as long as it is genuine, it is perhaps the most valuable quality any performer can have.

Musicians have an understandable fear of bad taste. But it is not always inappropriate. Not everyone shares Ravel's feeling that 'you do not have to open up your chest to prove you have a heart'. Mahler wanted music to express the whole world, a world at times as vulgar as it is sophisticated. As an objective in itself, good taste is unattainable, vanishing as instantly as water through a fork. Expressing yourself with it is imperative, but seeking to do so is dangerous. For there is a difference between manners and mannerisms. Taste is too personal to be studied yet also too important to be ignored. It is an essential ingredient, not an extra one – like the salt that releases the goodness of the food.

It is when it comes to taste that I think the greatest performances differ the most. I suspect this is because it is impossible to talk about it in rehearsal and trying to do so defeats even the most linguistically expert musicians. Yet precisely because conductors have to reveal their taste without words, the result is not limited by them. This particular communication between conductor and orchestra guarantees the uniqueness of each performance, a bond that rises above all the failings of musical notation and the inadequacies of verbal explanation.

There are some concerts where every note matters and every silence refocuses the intensity. Every nuance is explored, every shade coloured, every phrase sculpted, every rhythm danced, every line sung, every structure understood, and every drama acted out. The bold and the subtle receive equal value; emotions and logic are portrayed in perfect harmony, and an indefinable meaning and purpose swims alongside a simultaneously free-flowing spontaneity that relegates to the listener's subconscious the realisation that everything has been thought through. They do not happen often. They probably cannot happen often. But that does not diminish their value within your ambition.

4

Conducting Drama

Dare, always dare!
Lilian Baylis

In Richard Strauss's final opera, *Capriccio*, the heroine is wooed by a poet and a musician. The piece is a sensual dialectic exploring the relative value of words and music. By keeping the identity of the successful lover a secret, the point is symbolically made that it is impossible, and ultimately rather pointless, to decide between the two.

Music arouses in us a vast range of emotions. Words make them specific. Yet this specificity can be easily misunderstood. We have to think consciously about the words we hear – unlike the music – and this makes a listener's contribution to their meaning a significant part of the communication. Whether such explicit nature limits their depth or makes them more potent I am not sure. Prose moves fewer people to tears than music but it can still take your breath away. The greatest writers create mysterious sources of beauty and unending founts of inspiration, and 'limited' is hardly a word that springs to mind when thinking of Shakespeare, Tolstoy, or Keats. Hans Christian Andersen said that 'where words fail, music speaks', but when the singers explode out of the finale of Beethoven's Ninth Symphony, it sounds as if the opposite is true. Beethoven needed Schiller's text to make his point explicit. There's a sense of the meaning being extended rather than restricted and for many it is the enrichment that words and music bring to each other that offers the most complete expression. A song is the commonest form of artistic communication. With the voice of a great composer the message of music can be precise, and in the hands of a great writer the meaning of words is boundless. It is hardly surprising that combining them leads to the most powerful art form of all: opera.

*

The notion that opera is a glamorous and frivolous entertainment for the social and cultural elite may be a convenient stereotype, but for those who have experienced its power this couldn't be further from the truth. The vast majority of operas address subjects that are both real and relevant. Love, death, religion, sex, power, friendship, and betrayal are primal concerns of the human condition and to hear them expressed through the elemental voices of music and drama is to make a connection with their significance that is profound and thrilling. Operatic music is instantly recognisable as such – even the purely orchestral sections. Its sound world wears its humanity on its sleeve with the directness of a spotlight and the vivid intensity of theatrical make-up. It seems to smell of greasepaint. But there is also a fragility to its perfume that reflects the nakedness of such emotional vulnerability. Operas force the performers to bare their souls in a far more open way than symphonies do. You cannot pretend you are not exploring deeply personal issues.

The differences between symphonic and operatic conducting are considerable, and I am glad to be able to perform both in equal measure. Nevertheless, it can be easy to succumb to the grass-is-greener syndrome. As the unsympathetic clock ticks down at the end of an opera rehearsal that can involve over 250 people, all of whom are looking to the conductor to provide the time for them to be able to solve their own particular problems, it is tempting to wish for the much simpler symphonic scenario in which you are significantly more in control of the means of meeting any of the purely musical challenges you and the orchestra face. But at exactly the same point in the preparation for a concert, one can long for the much greater sense of shared responsibility that so many people bring to an operatic project.

The sheer number of performers involved in opera makes the experience extremely engaging on a human level and, though the conductor is officially responsible only for how the music sounds, it is impossible to meet that responsibility without reference to what the set looks like, how the staging affects the singers' ability to sing, what they are wearing, how they are lit and, most important of all, what are the dramatic choices that have been made that determine every character and situation. Ideally, everyone is seeking the same end but, whether that is the case or not, the conductor is not the only one in charge. That can be hard to handle if this is something you find threatening on a personal level, but it is this essential collaboration that makes an operatic undertaking so rewarding. Getting exactly what you want might sound attractive, but it's not as meaningful as achieving something with other people, even if you have to compromise on specific wishes in order to do so.

The amount of effort that goes into an opera performance is considerable. Sharing that effort with so many people is inspiring and fulfilling. Of course, musicians in a symphony orchestra care equally deeply, but from the conductor's standpoint there is a greater anonymity to that care. The passion expressed by opera is by its very nature more personal, and those on stage have to take a very public ownership of what that passion is. The opera conductor does not feel alone when the exposure of performing is so generously shared.

As well as the benefits of working with so many other people in the theatre, another significant advantage that opera has over the symphonic world comes simply from the time you all spend working together on any particular piece. The customary two or three days of rehearsal for a concert creates a pressure for the conductor to be able to generate a musical relationship with an orchestra almost instantaneously, as well as a necessity to be far more assertive about the musical decisions that have to be taken. These time constraints make it harder for the process to be as collaborative as one might like, although an ability to quick-fix suits some conductors' personalities and skills more than others. Opera rehearsal periods vary hugely, depending on the circumstances of the event, but though the differences can be considerable, you still spend far more time with an opera than you do with a symphony. By the first performance of an opera production you could very well have conducted some sections of the piece, with either a rehearsal piano or an orchestra, a hundred times or more. And despite a first night's theatrical sense of occasion, and a heightened expectation that is the culmination of several weeks' preparation, on a purely musical level I am normally relatively relaxed. The number of rehearsals has allowed me to try a great many possibilities, and as a result I find it much easier to be musically convinced and therefore physically confident of what I am doing.

★

There is a curious tension in today's operatic culture between the musical priority of the performers, which typically tries to be one of complete fidelity to the composer's instructions, and the dramatic one, where the philosophy is that a piece is a springboard for a director's limitless imagination. One sees the score as the end, the other as the beginning. Taken to extremes, both views are wrong. The score is a source of expression, not a rigid framework within which every performer has to conform, but the visual and dramatic choices have to come from something that is audible, and in that sense there is a margin outside which some theatrical ideas cannot work. This margin is wide, though. Just as the greatest symphonies have many plausible interpretations, so too do the greatest operas. The success of the interpretation depends on the motivation of those making the decisions.

Although there are opera productions I have seen, and even conducted, that I feel contradict the dramatic intentions of the composer, I am always happy to defend the right of directors to make their choices. Despite the unlikelihood of being persuaded that setting *Madama Butterfly* on the moon is finally going to reveal the work's true meaning, I believe it is the wide variety of dramatic interpretations that is currently keeping opera alive. In the absence of a mainstream audience's curiosity for new repertoire, the allure of any new production of a well-known work lies primarily in what is going to happen theatrically rather than musically. I don't think it is a coincidence that the role of a director became significant only once it was clear that the public no longer felt that motivated by contemporary work. When there was more appeal through the novelty of the pieces themselves, only the designer and the stage manager took much responsibility for what a performance looked like. But now that many people more or less know what they expect to hear in the music, it is the director's influence on the production that intrigues many of them in the first place.

Some people say they prefer 'traditional' productions. I never really know what they mean by that. Looking at pictures of the clichéd costumes and archaic sets of nineteenth-century Wagnerian performances, I presume that is not what they are referring to. One can have enough of men in tights. Our visual and dramatic sensibilities have changed even more than our musical ones, and to put on exact copies of original productions would be laughable nowadays. That doesn't mean *The Marriage of Figaro* cannot take place in eighteenth-century Vienna or that *Aida* has to be set in ancient Egypt. There are good and bad productions, not right and wrong ones.

I think three time periods are easily defendable for any operatic staging: the date the piece is meant to be set (controversial, I know), the date it was written, or today. Although there are some notable exceptions that have disproved this philosophy, and I am happy to be persuaded by directors who offer a convincing case for whatever they want to do, on the whole a period setting outside these three options feels to me an imposition rather than a revelation. As a comparison, conductors might argue for using instruments of the composer's time or they might want a more contemporary orchestral sound but it would be considered a gross affectation to attempt to create anything in between. It would be hard to imagine a conductor asking orchestra musicians playing Mozart to sound as if they were performing it in the 1920s.

There does not, however, always have to be unanimity between the auditory and the visual. If done well, a contradiction between them can be very stimulating and throw new light on both what is heard and what is seen. Dissonance can be just as successful as consonance. As long as the director 'hears' the voice of the composer, the conscious decision to offset the musical implications can be very powerful, especially when everyone involved believes in what they are doing. The directors who inspire me the most are not the ones who *stage* exactly what is written in the score but the ones who *know* exactly what is written in the score. Opera is not a play with music. Nor is it a concert in fancy dress. The issues it raises can often even be dis*concert*ing. Some people enjoy opera as a purely auditory experience, but that is not what the composers want. They make a decision to create a work for the theatre. They want to write a dramatic work and they expect it to be engaged with on this level at least as much as it is on a musical one. Operas need both the conductor and director to honour that combination.

A relationship between a conductor and a director is often intense. This is not so much due to the egos of those involved – both are well versed in working with confident people – but because an opera makes so many demands of both a musical and a dramatic nature that the leader of each wants to prioritise the efforts that serve their own specific department. The best conductors and directors care about their work a great deal. In isolation that care can be limitless, but collaboration halves the time available while simultaneously doubling the complexity of the project. It is a pressurised situation that mutual respect goes a long way to releasing. If the conductor is interested in the drama and the director is interested in the music, the singers are empowered to deliver both with equal commitment and the audience will experience the work of the composer and librettist without any disconnect between them.

Of course, there can be artistic tensions. Conductors and directors need each other to deliver their own vision for the piece and if they cannot share a single vision, the compromises are stressful and disappointing for everyone. Both are employed to persuade the performers to buy into their opinions. If singers find themselves pulled in two different directions, the creative process is never going to be satisfying. That is why the first and foremost responsibility of the conductor and the director is to agree with each other. If the two individuals concerned are sufficiently confident to welcome interpretative discussion, you get a stimulating working environment that undoubtedly leads to the best result – that leads in fact to opera: a medium in which music and drama have an invisible and indivisible connection, neither dominating at the expense of the other, both able to lead without either being left behind.

There's nothing wrong with a bit of friction, though. If a conductor can challenge directors into making choices that they would not have discovered on their own, and if the directors do the same in return, each will have benefited from the other's influence. The director will have taken decisions that allow singers to sing better and the conductor made choices that allow them to act better. For this to happen, both conductor and director need to be at all the rehearsals. In the old days, conductors would lead the first two days of the rehearsal period so that everyone would know what the 'master of ceremonies' required. The conductor would then disappear, returning only once the orchestra arrived, relatively late in the process, expecting none of the staging rehearsals that had been happening in the meantime to have affected the music in any way. Given that the director would not have been present at the initial music rehearsals, it was possible for conductor and director never to meet. Fortunately, this absurd state of dysfunction very rarely occurs today, though I did meet a director recently who half an hour into our conversation told me that this was the longest time he had ever talked to a conductor.

Most conductors want to be present most of the time. We want to influence with our own view of the drama, and to be able to factor the director's and the singers' thoughts into our musical ideas. Conductors control the dramatic pacing during the performance but the only way that you can also embrace the views of the other people involved is to be at every rehearsal. The traditional opera rehearsal system would often keep the conductor and director apart. But this is hardly conducive to collaboration, and it is not surprising that opera developed a reputation among some for a performance aesthetic in which the powerful connection between music and drama was often diluted by the dominance of one or the other. Opera asks the audience to sense no difference between music and drama. That is hard if the rehearsal structure has made such a difference abundantly clear.

One could argue that the relationship between music and drama in the performance of an opera should be the same as that between composer and librettist during its creation. There is no doubt who is in charge. The words might be written first but composers get the top billing and will not hesitate to ask for changes should the text deviate from their musical vision for the story. I imagine most directors would be against such a hierarchy, and given that in only a few circumstances do opera companies decide on a conductor before they choose the director, the operatic priorities of our time are clear. But the best directors know that if their dramatic ideas are not underpinned by musical conviction, their productions will not be truly successful. After all, it is the conductor, not the director, who is involved in the actual performance itself.

★

A conductor's structural pacing of an opera in both a detailed and an overarching sense is what allows the drama to unfold with the right intensity at the right time. The need to guide the emotional narrative is the same as it is in a symphony but it is far easier to do this in an opera, where the story leaves little to the imagination as to what that structural journey is. It is hard to disagree that the first time Mimi and Rodolfo touch hands in *La bohème* should be a moment of increased intensity, and you don't have to be an interpretative genius to appreciate the musical significance needed to accompany the moment Carmen is stabbed, Tosca jumps off the ramparts, or Don Giovanni is dragged down to hell. But what does make conducting the structure harder in opera is that the visible communicators of its highs and lows are the singers themselves. Influencing them from twenty yards away in the pit can be difficult, and when it comes to the performance not even necessarily desirable.

As far as the audience is concerned the drama takes place on the stage and it has to be perceived as being led from there. Yet, because the conductor is the only person involved in every moment of every scene, you are the one who sustains the journey of the whole piece. Your 'accompaniment' needs to be profoundly influential, even if that influence is mainly directed towards empowering the singers to lead rather than to follow. Wagner understood this contradiction. Even though he gave the weight of the emotional expression to the orchestra and hence the responsibility for it to the conductor, he designed his theatre at Bayreuth to hide both from the audience. It might look as if the singers are in charge theatrically but the orchestra is the invisible source of the drama. It is the perfect combination: a private orchestra leading a public singer. There is a recognition that our invisible souls are in charge of the actions and reactions of our hearts and minds. This is a particularly Wagnerian concept and it isn't necessarily the right model for every opera, but the delicate balance between following and leading is the basis of all conducting, and how you achieve this in opera depends on the piece and the conventions of the time and place for which it was written.

Up until Mozart's time, operas would revolve around a combination of recitatives that delivered the action and a series of arias in which the characters reflected on what and how they were feeling. The timing of the recitatives, in which the orchestra is not involved, is beyond a conductor's control, at least in performance. There is a sense in which even the composer takes a back seat, re-grabbing the reins only once the orchestra strikes up again. But even the arias of these early operas demand a relatively passive contribution from the conductor. The very nature of a *da capo* aria, in which the first half is repeated, albeit with ornamental variety, suggests a certain stasis. Not that that is unrealistic – the idea of engaging in one particular emotion for a specific and even extended period of time is very believable – but it requires from the conductor an expressive skill that is more reflective than dramatic.

Singing reveals text with its fullest range of dramatic expression. The orchestra allows a composer to enrich it still further and in some cases to go deeper than even the characters on stage are aware. In Mozart's *Così fan tutte*, for instance, Fiordiligi is convinced she loves Guglielmo but the music in the orchestra makes it clear to the audience that she probably shouldn't be so sure of herself. The idea that, through the orchestra, a composer can express more than the characters themselves is what allows opera to be such a rich medium and, despite its image to the contrary, potentially even more realistic an expression of a dramatic situation than purely spoken theatre.

It was Mozart's introduction of more ensemble-based dramatic situations that generated the practical need for these ensembles to be 'managed', and his investing the orchestra with a greater sense of dramatic and emotional commentary that necessitated the performance being unified by a single person. Mozart's love of the ensemble – trios, quartets, quintets, sextets, and beyond – was to some degree a musical thrill in expressing a variety of emotions simultaneously, but it was mainly a dramatic device for furthering the action through the orchestrated music and not just through the recitatives. The result was the birth of the opera conductor – someone who must be sensitive to the length of time characters need to express themselves as well as to the speed that situations require to be dramatically credible. The final twenty minutes of any of the operas that Mozart wrote with the librettist Lorenzo Da Ponte demand a carefully graded ebb and flow of excitement and tension that is pretty much the constant role of the conductor for most of the operas that followed.

Simplistically speaking, nineteenth-century operas can be divided into those in which the orchestra takes the lead and those in which the voice is more in charge. With the more Germanic line of Wagner and Strauss the dramatic tension essentially comes from the pit. The conductor can manage the emotional journey through an orchestral point of view. The Italian school of Bellini, Donizetti, and Verdi on the other hand demands a vocal impetus for the action. If you listen to Wagner without the singers you miss the humanity of the voice but not the personality of the drama. Verdi without the orchestra diminishes the depth of the characters but not their motivation. Of course, the singing in Wagner is just as important as the orchestra is in Verdi, but the two approaches need two very different types of conducting. Some conductors are happier in one or other of the styles but for many of us it is an impossible 'Sophie's Choice'.

Debussy said that the problem with Italian opera is that the orchestra is always waiting for the singer and the problem with German opera is that the singer is always waiting for the orchestra. He and contemporaries such as Janáček and Berg sought to merge the two into a more indivisible relationship. Their operas mostly take place in real time and were you to speak the texts without the music they would pretty much last as long as the operas do. For the conductor this makes them the easiest to pace dramatically. You can be confident that what is true for the text will be true for the music and therefore what feels right for the orchestra is similarly going to be an ideal representation of the drama. With operas such as *Pelléas et Mélisande*, *Jenůfa*, or *Wozzeck*, the marriage between music and drama is so perfect that the composer has made the conductor's job easy. It is like directing *Hamlet* with Shakespeare telling you exactly when and how to deliver each line. Nothing is ever as simple as just doing what it says on the page, but if that is indeed all and exactly what you do, you will have got pretty close to the truth without the need for much imaginative second-guessing.

One of the interesting things about performing opera is that no decisions can be taken in isolation. How the music should sound depends on the dramatic energy of the situation, the age of the characters, and the place each scene has within the significance of the whole. In return, all these choices can be based on the evidence of the music. Both music and drama come with a great many possibilities. Preparing a score in advance of an opera rehearsal process is about discovering those possibilities rather than deciding on them. Assuming there is sufficient rehearsal time, this set of options then gets refined into a unified whole. Every choice sets up musical and dramatic consequences that need to be followed through and operas offer a labyrinth of opportunities to take the wrong turnings. Success comes from everyone remaining open to exploring which paths are the best ones to take and no one's vanity being put out if it becomes apparent that a wrong choice has been made. A director might have a good idea that does not actually sound very good. A conductor might imagine a phrasing that contradicts the singer's dramatic intentions. On their own, few choices are right or wrong. But there is a distinction between true and false, and only in rehearsal can you discover the connections that allow you to find the right solution for the particular group of people involved.

An audience can tell whether everyone is taking part in the same performance or not and it is for all to commit to whatever that unified vision implies.

★

There is always a frisson on the first day of an opera rehearsal – a feeling that anything, and everything, is possible. There is a great deal of bonhomie, sincere in its eagerness to create a good working atmosphere for a period that can sometimes last as long as a couple of months. But there is also a certain amount of tacit apprehension and insecurity. The vulnerability is understandable. Everyone arrives knowing only part of the story – like spies who have had only a bit of the truth revealed to them. The singers know their parts – normally – but not the director's understanding of them. The conductor has a sense of the character of each role but perhaps not whether a singer will agree with that view. I have found singers vary far more than instrumentalists in that regard. Every musician is unique, but when the instrument is an external one, it is not as directly connected to the personality of the player as the voice is to the singer. This can make it harder for singers to adapt to something without sounding disingenuous. Professionals of course try their best to do what the conductor or director asks but if they don't think an interpretation is valid, it is tougher for singers to set aside their doubts than it is for instrumentalists. The audience reacts more humanly too and can more readily spot a fake and imposed interpretation in an opera than in a symphony. Singers know this. Their nerves at the start of rehearsals are caused not by a lack of confidence in their ability but by the possibility they might be asked to do something they don't believe in. It has been known.

Conductors want singers, even more than they do orchestras, to take ownership of a specific musical interpretation. Yet singers are also soloists, and because they sing arias as well as duets, trios, and larger ensembles, their personalities have to enjoy expressing their ego as much as their more collaborative qualities. It's not an uncomplicated combination. Instrumental soloists can afford to be relatively determined in achieving their musical goal. The nature of a concerto makes it abundantly clear that there is an individual dynamic in apposition to a group dynamic and it is for the conductor to marry the two together. Opera singers are soloists at any point in which they are singing but most operas involve a variety of people on stage at once and how these characters interact with each other creates the drama of the situation. They cannot simply do their own thing. That's not always easy for personalities who need an extraordinary amount of self-confidence to do what they do in the first place.

Compared with instrumentalists, singers commit to music relatively late in their lives. For many, their voice doesn't develop until their early twenties. They might well have learned an instrument in childhood, and you hear the disciplined musicianship of those that have, but a desire to be an opera singer often blossoms only well after personalities have already been formed. The musical issues that arise from this unusual timing are for the most part easy for them to deal with, but embracing everything else they have to do can be a problematic psychological adjustment. Most opera singers were far from stagestruck children with Mrs Worthingtons for mothers, and as adult performers many come to the stage with a certain reluctance. Despite its reputation as a big gesture, ('operatic' is not always a compliment), opera is an intimate and personal form of expression. And often a large orchestra and an even larger stage require a heightened intensity to this sincerity. To make opera work its characters need to believe that what they have to say is so important that it has to be sung.

Perhaps because of the contrast between musical confidence and dramatic insecurity, singers are often far more open to directors than they are to conductors. In fact, I am fascinated that they will accept being asked to sing upside-down, scantily dressed, with a heavy wig, and their backs to the audience, yet are sometimes reluctant to sing at an ever so slightly different speed from the one they prepared. It is almost enough to make you want to be a director and not a conductor. But then a chorus of eighty singers comes on stage needing to look realistic yet choreographed and you understand why many directors would like what they perceive to be the easier job of conducting.

Conductors expect singers to express in public real emotions that the text and dramatic situation make explicit. We ask them to sing, dance, act, feel, emote, think, count, remember, listen, commit, and collaborate. We want them to be egocentric while claiming responsibility for an interpretation they might not agree with, and we need them to do all this however they may be feeling physically at the time. As a result, the professional relationship between a singer and a conductor is often the most demanding and rewarding one they each have. Without any help or detraction from anything other than their own body and soul, the nakedness of this connection creates tremendous tension and power. It is unsurprising many have taken their relationship as far as the altar.

The vulnerability of the human voice is one of the main sources of its power, and this power is the greatest one there is in music. For as long as there have been professional musicians, singers have been the superstars. What must be the oldest form of music-making resonates deep within our past. And when it is used to articulate the most human of emotions, it is very hard to have an ambivalent reaction. The popularity of singers is not simply that the wide range of repertoire available to them provides an opportunity to touch so many. The prejudice behind the term 'cross-over' when used to describe the boundaries between classical and popular music speaks for itself, but a more apt application of the phrase would be to describe crossing over the boundary between performer and listener. Voices do that not only because everybody can to a certain extent sing but because singing encourages humanity – a sense of the music being more than just music, more than just what it is expressing. It generates a bond with the listener that is stronger than just art.

Conductors, like singers, have no external instrument and use only their bodies to express the music. Every other musician speaks through an instrument, but these channels for musical communication can also be a barrier to the public's perception of them on a personal level. With singers and conductors, the public has no alternative but to engage with their personal identities. People are quick to criticise the egos of both, but they would disapprove even more quickly if the performers had none. Egocentricity doesn't have to express itself with arrogance or selfishness, but the self-confidence required to reveal so much of one's self cannot be denied.

*

Singers are the visible stars of an opera performance, but there is not a single opera in which the orchestra does not have the main role. It is playing all the time, expressing each character's thoughts and feelings, giving depth to the sets and colour to the lighting. Even in *bel canto* operas such as *Norma* or *Lucia di Lammermoor*, where the voices are the more overt protagonists, the soul of the characters and the essence of any dramatic tension and resolution comes from below the stage rather than on it. In fact, this power is intensified precisely because the source of it is hidden. The absence of any personal connection between the audience and the instrumentalists enables the music to work its magic in a subliminal way. The subconscious becomes more available the less the conscious is engaged by an orchestra's physical dimension. Wagner knew that the musicians needed to be shielded from view if they were to be able to influence an audience as deeply as he sought. For him, the orchestra was the essence of the drama, and like any good magician he wanted the tricks of his trade to be concealed.

Playing in an opera-house pit has its challenges. The grimness of most of them is a stark contrast to the glamour of the theatre itself. It is usually cramped; it is always dark; it can be hard to hear the singers, and the musicians rarely have a sense of how their playing comes across to the audience. Add to that the fact that almost every opera is significantly longer than almost every symphony, and that you are performing most nights of the week, and one wonders how anyone survives. Yet some of the most fulfilled musicians I know are the ones who play opera. Ask them what it is like to perform the fifteen hours of Wagner's *Ring*, and invariably a look of dreamy privilege crosses over them. Certainly more than when asked about any symphony by Beethoven, Brahms, or Mahler. I have not yet met a musician who is bored by one of the Mozart–Da Ponte operas.

This may be because there are fewer standard operas than there are standard symphonies. The repertoire is smaller and consequently repeated more often. The need to rehearse an opera for more than just the orchestra's benefit means that the musicians' understanding of each piece is incredibly deep. The sense of ownership this instils is a great source of pride to opera orchestras, and though it can create a challenge for a conductor who wants to do something other than the norm, such knowledge and experience is predominantly a powerful force for good.

Any potential for boredom engendered by the limited repertoire is offset by the fact that the theatricality of the music widens the variety of approach, and the broad range of personalities that sing each role helps avoid the danger of repetition. Every Don Giovanni will sound different, and even the same singers can sound different on any given night. The voice is so connected to its owner's health and well-being that rarely is any performance exactly the same. Good opera orchestras adapt to anything that a singer does as long as it stays within the limits that their experience has led them to understand as necessary. Those in the pit know when a singer chooses a path that will turn out to be a cul-de-sac. Their consciousness of what will work and what will not is something that a conductor does well to trust.

The fact that the orchestra is only part of an operatic experience might be one of the reasons why many players love it. It is in most people's nature to want to be part of something and an opera company gives all involved a feeling that they are working towards a goal they could never achieve alone. On a good night, the sense of 'company' that runs through a performance is rich and gives the musical experience a social context and a human connection that cannot be matched by any symphony. Orchestra musicians are not by and large the most egocentric of people. By playing in an orchestra they are demonstrating their enthusiasm to be part of something bigger than themselves, and by belonging to an opera company, that sense of belonging is intensified tenfold.

Despite the drawbacks of playing in the pit, there can be something wonderful about not being seen by the audience. For orchestra players, knowing that it is only what they sound like that matters can liberate them from any sensitivities about how they might look when they play. The best opera orchestras don't take that as an invitation to be sloppy. They do look uniform. It's just that this is a result of seeking a musical unity rather than a visual one. Free from a relatively meaningless need to look good, they can focus purely on the aural element of their work. This is true for a conductor as well. Although most of the time it's easy to ignore the self-consciousness that one can feel from a concert audience, your visual anonymity in opera affords the opportunity for total concentration on the music and the musicians. The subterranean depths filter out, or at least dilute, any potential for visual distraction, and to a certain extent they protect you from audible distractions as well.

Having said that, the design of most opera-house auditoriums makes the orchestra and conductor a very real presence and in theatrical terms this causes significant challenges. Neither orchestra nor conductor are a visual part of the drama, and even with the most sunken pits there is a physical gap that needs to be bridged if the audience is going to feel connected to the characters on the stage. If you believe that opera is a form of theatre, the concept of dividing the stage and the auditorium is problematic, and it can be difficult for directors and conductors to marry the emotional and physical presence of the orchestra to the purely dramatic needs of the story as a whole. What is an orchestra doing on a beach in *Peter Grimes*? How can Aida's tomb feel lonely and isolated when there appears to be room for seventy-five musicians as well? I am being obtuse, but a Stanislavskian truthfulness is hard to conjure alongside the musical need for the conductor and singer to be able to see each other. If you cannot see the singers, you cannot follow their lead, and if they cannot see you, they cannot follow yours. A good opera performance, just like any symphonic one, is a synchronicity of conductors, singers, and instrumentalists leading and following each other without any predetermined hierarchy. There is a mutual consideration that makes it impossible to tell who is in charge, a unanimity of emotional temperature, and an inevitable but seemingly unique sense of direction.

Assuming you have a love of drama, and I'm not sure why you would be conducting an opera if you did not, the dramatic context of every bar makes its musical meaning considerably easier to understand than it is with the more abstract nature of concert music. The human specifics are incontestable. You could tell a symphony orchestra that you think a passage in a Beethoven symphony should sound like a love affair doomed by fate and the musicians could think, 'Well, maybe; maybe not.' But in an opera this is not a matter of opinion. The text is the text, and though it can have many degrees of subtlety, you are in a position to back up your requests with the libretto's proof of their validity. It is hard for orchestra musicians to question being asked to play with more attack in their sound at the moment that Tristan is stabbed with a sword. If they know that the opening scene of *Der Rosenkavalier* takes place in a post-coital bedroom, they are more likely to give its prelude an appropriate level of physical passion. Involving the orchestra in the drama is essential if you are going to ask them to express it and most musicians enjoy having the clarity of a musical idea defined to them through the extra-musical dynamics of the scene itself.

Notwithstanding the significance and purpose of an opera's orchestra, it is still the human voice that provides its distinctive sound. The voice's ability to move us is so strong that almost all music aspires towards a vocal quality. Conductors are constantly asking orchestras to make their instruments 'sing', whatever form of music they are playing, but opera orchestras hear the sound of the voice every day. A sense of the breath, a *legato* line, and a natural rise and fall of melody are an audible concomitant to their working life. For them, music's human quality is second nature. It is in all the pieces they play and all the singers they accompany, and when you have an orchestra with lyricism in its ears and drama in its heart, two of the most important responsibilities of a conductor are taken care of. There are undoubted practical complexities of conducting opera but at a most basic level its challenges are met instinctively by many of the opera orchestras in the world.

★

The earliest operas were essentially chamber operas. They were written to be performed in relatively small rooms, certainly compared with most opera houses of today. A room is a space for thoughts not speeches, for direct eye contact rather than extravagant hand gestures, and the absence of a large audience would have created an intensely private and powerful experience. Opera's journey towards grandiosity arose purely from the vanity of its patrons, who vied with each other to promote ever more splendid occasions, a competitive spirit that still leads many artistic choices around the world today. But whereas in the past aristocratic courts used opera as an opportunity to show how much money they had, nowadays the costs that arise from whatever decisions are made get passed on to the public in some form or other. Opera has thus become expensive, and the inevitable tag of elitism follows closely behind. The art form itself is not the problem; it is the fact that only a very small section of society thinks it can afford it. If the financial implications of artistic profligacy on the stage preclude diversity in the auditorium, the relevance of opera in the future will become profoundly threatened.

The gap between opera and the performance of opera has become a wide one. All the paraphernalia that now goes with it – social, financial, political – distracts from the experience itself. The most successful opera companies today are the ones that place as many of their resources as possible on the people who directly affect the public's experience, trusting the human connection that audiences seek. Opera is at its best when it is as it was originally meant to be: an intimate and precise combination of words and music that uses a dramatic context to reveal the human condition. It is a simplicity that unlocks an unfathomable range of emotions. Complicating that simplicity can show a lack of faith in the work that has confusing consequences for an audience. And if the cost of such elaboration makes it less attractive to the curious, it really is a lose–lose situation.

All art is irrational. That is its purpose. Rationality is for real life, a life that is nonetheless limited if it does not explore the irrational as well. We need both. Given that we don't sing to each other that often, opera is particularly irrational. But this is one of its greatest strengths. The ubiquity of operatic surtitles, however, encourages a literal approach, and despite their benefits, the danger is that opera's more elemental power is diminished. Leaving aside the fact that it is hard to truly listen and read at the same time, or that the eye cannot look in two places at once, or that the specific timing of the delivery of the text is no longer up to the performer, by giving our conscious so much power over our subconscious we negate opera's ability to transport us beyond the here and now. Surtitles also offer an opportunity for performers to abdicate some of their own responsibilities. I have had a director say to me that it doesn't matter if such and such a line is not reflected in the staging because it will not be put up on the surtitles, and I have heard a singer say that diction is no longer important because this is not how the text is being communicated. But if that is the level of sincerity and commitment coming off the stage, it is very hard to demand the same from your audience. This lack of trust in opera is rare. Five minutes in most rehearsal rooms would disabuse anyone of the notion that there is a desire to create something vague and superficial. An enormous amount of hard work, talent, passion, collaboration, and respect goes into making something true, powerful, and unique.

The history of opera shows that the leadership of its performance has always been weighted towards one particular component. Once there was singer-opera. The advent of recording turned that into conductor-opera. A search for greater theatricality then led to director-opera. Nowadays the person with the most power is likely to be neither a singer nor a conductor nor a director. This is not necessarily a problem if that person understands what everybody involved in the performances needs to do. In principle, an overview that balances all the artistic components equally is appropriate. But if a project's only objective is to be within its budget, the entire budget is a waste of money. The only justification for the expense of opera is that it offers more value than cost. If you do not believe in that value, it is always going to seem too expensive. Success should not be measured by whether you survive or not, and those that think survival is success enough are not supporting opera's long-term interests. Of course, artists have to work within the financial parameters of their company, just as tennis players have to hit the ball within the lines. Those are the rules. But you are not going to win many matches if that is your only goal. If opera is going to remain relevant to the society it should reflect, challenge, and inspire, it needs to speak a contemporary language that does justice to that relevance. And it needs to speak it with self-belief. Competition for audiences has never been stronger. People have the right to the highest musical quality, and the most exciting drama. Anything less has no right to an audience.

There are a great number of things that can go wrong in an opera performance. This understanding doesn't diminish your ambition but, rather, embraces your aspiration with a healthy sense of perspective. You might well start conducting a Brahms symphony attempting a definitive performance on every occasion. Whether this even exists is debatable, but nobody expects such a thing in the opera house. A knowledge of the inevitable unpredictability of the journey offers an openness that is extremely exciting and present. Yet every now and again everything does go right. The singers, orchestra, backstage technicians, conductor, and audience all surpass what they had expected of themselves and of others, and just for a handful of evenings in your life the intense hard work that everyone has put in on their own and as a group realises its dream. It is rare that the ultimate art form produces an ultimate performance. But those lucky enough to have been part of one are privileged beyond compare.

5

Conducting Performances

We had the experience but missed the meaning.
T. S. Eliot, *The Cocktail Party*

The earliest physical evidence of music-making dates back to some 36,000-year-old bone flutes found in Germany and France. As singing would have most likely preceded the crafting of any instruments, we can safely assume that musical behaviour has been part of who we are for a very long time. Every culture in the world makes music, and for many societies it is as vital as speech. Indeed, the theory that language is an offshoot of music, rather than the other way round, is compelling, and those who believe that the complexity of music was a contributory factor in the brain development of early humans illustrate their arguments with the fact that we sing to our children from their very first day. Speaking to babies with a 'musically' exaggerated sense of rise and fall suggests an instinctive understanding of music's deep-rooted power to communicate.

Like language itself, music is part of being human. The fact that we are the only species that creates music, at least in the way we generally understand such a form of organised sound, invites the question whether or not music is an evolutionary adaptation, and if it is, what do we gain from it. Charles Darwin thought that music preceded speech and in his book *The Descent of Man* wrote that our early musical capacities were akin to birdsong 'first acquired by the male or female progenitors of mankind for the sake of charming the opposite sex'. On the other hand, Herbert Spencer, who was actually the first to coin the phrase 'survival of the fittest', suggested that it was emotional speech that led to music. Jean-Jacques Rousseau, conveniently a composer as well as a philosopher, simply believed they emerged together. Some academics view music as an evolutionary by-product with no special significance for human survival, but many others think that it is far more profound than the 'auditory cheesecake' label applied to it by the popular science writer Steven Pinker.

Whatever the role of music might have been in the past, many people's experience of it now is completely different from that of our ancestors and, in Western classical music at least, a divide between performers and listeners has become dangerously distinct. Players are viewed as a specialised minority and audiences are increasingly self-deprecating about their own musical abilities. Even the word 'ability' has been hijacked to imply talent or skill. We almost all have the capability to make music but society has added such a value to what it should sound like that many people feel too inhibited to express themselves with it. A hundred years ago, music lovers would have been asked what instrument they played. Today the question is more likely to be about what they like listening to. Yet in some cultures the difference between playing and listening is much vaguer. Music is viewed as a language that everyone participates in, and to say someone is tone deaf is akin to saying that they cannot speak. Amusia is in fact a rare clinical condition. It seems we are almost all musical.

Music has long been a crucial part of social cohesion. Whether we are in church, at a sports stadium, or even at a birthday party, singing celebrates bonds that strengthen individual and group identities through a sharing of information and memories. Dancing is also a fundamental way we use music to connect and it is not surprising that this feels such a primal thing to do. Music's rhythmic energy activates our motor neurones and when simultaneously shared by others, this synchronicity reinforces powerful connections. Singing and dancing are not just a celebration of life, but of togetherness – a unison formed by doing not by listening. The more passive our approach to music is, the less collective the experience will be. And if the original purpose of music was a communal one, experiencing it in a more private scenario is perhaps limited and unnatural.

An active relationship to music has to be established at an early age, and I think children who are encouraged to think of music as something you do, that anyone can do, will discover its purpose and pleasure without judgement or prejudice. They will realise that music is not just a hobby for the periphery of life but a form of expression that combines the physical and the emotional, the intellectual and the spiritual, the social and the individual, connecting everyone on the planet with an extraordinary combination of the simple and the complex. Music is for all of us. It is about all of us.

Just as it is considered more relevant that children play sport rather than watch it, so too should they first be exposed to music as something they do rather than something they listen to. It is ironic that such a goal-orientated activity as sport promotes the view that it is more important to take part than to win, whereas despite the impossibility of any sort of victory in music, there's a feeling that you have to achieve a certain standard to enjoy it. And it doesn't help that if you aspire to be the best at sport, your ambition is considered impressive, while the pride that creative people have is often judged as elitist in some derogatory way. There is undoubtedly a competitive aspect to the music business, but it is always an artificial imposition onto music itself.

Those within classical music who are employed to reach out to as many people as possible know that simply getting more children to come to performances will not instil in them a lifelong love of music that reaps rewards in the future. What matters is not how many young people go to concerts but how many of them are playing instruments. It is a personal connection that waters the shoots of musical curiosity that only later grow into seeking out the joys of listening as well as playing.

We are not going to go back to the days when families would spend their evenings singing around the piano. But the more actively involved with music we are, the greater its benefits. By going to a live concert, our 'participation' in the performance plays a crucial part in the act, and therefore the survival, of music-making. Yet, for a variety of reasons, fewer people are making such a choice. Everyone in the music business is aware of this, but there are many different opinions as to its causes and how the challenges it presents should be met.

Our digital age grants us almost unlimited access to music. The benefits of technology are obvious, but in the long run the opportunity for music to be ubiquitous threatens its essential *raison d'être*. In the nineteenth century, listening to music was a special occasion. It was rarely heard by accident. But what emerged in the twentieth century, through a desire to extend the reach of music's beauty and meaning, could in the twenty-first century force us to become so sanitised to its sounds that we lose the ability to enjoy it at all. Too much light, and no one can see the stars. The wide availability of music is not the issue. It is how rarely we can escape from it that causes a problem. More often than not, going out in public is to be accompanied by an endless, undiluted soundtrack over which private thoughts struggle to be heard among the multitude of melodies forced on us. Listening to music should be an active choice, not an Orwellian design to keep us quiet. Silence is not a void, but a space – a space that everyone has a right to control.

The only way to deal with incessant onslaughts to our aural senses is to develop a means of being unaffected by them. Many people no longer notice background music and a generation is growing up believing that a constant stream of notes buzzing through a solitary earpiece is part of a contemporary uniform it cannot do without. But the ability to carry on normal conversation at the same time suggests that we have developed the capacity to hear without listening. Given that 15 per cent of young people are reported to have hearing difficulties, this might prove to be an unfortunate maladaptation. Listening engages both the brain and the heart within a specific cultural context unique to every one of us. But by being forced so often to hear music passively, we risk losing our capability, or even our inclination, to listen to it actively.

I don't think it helps that some of the established traditions of live classical music contribute to deactivating the listener. Nineteenth-century Romanticism elevated the performer from courtly servant to exotic hero. The likes of Paganini and Liszt were exceptional people but by putting performers on a pedestal, literally in the case of the conductors, lines between 'them' and 'us' became more sharply drawn. The journey from the minstrel's gallery to the decorum of modern-day concert halls is essentially beneficial. But discouraging audiences from participating in the performance can lead to a dangerous disconnect between listener and player. It is perhaps to be expected that some in the audience feel alienated from the experience.

Musicians need to be intensely conscious of the potential drawbacks of the situations we have created for ourselves, but devaluing the sense of occasion will certainly not help increase its popularity. There is a difference between art and entertainment. Art raises ideas that entertainment encourages us to ignore; classical musicians can be proud that audiences need to work harder for one than the other. Proud because we believe the reward is proportionally much greater. But our efforts to make something exceptional must not contradict our desire to speak to the reality of our time. Audiences are as much a part of the occasion as musicians. Once we asked them not to be, and pressurised them into being passive admirers, we made them feel anonymous, and opened the door to the possibility of thinking the experience is not relevant to them.

A concert hall offers a controlled sense of peace and stability within what can be a hectic and chaotic world. Most of us lead lives bombarded by random activity and insignificant information. We rarely sit and do nothing, simply listening, feeling, thinking. To give oneself the opportunity to abandon everyday reality, forcing the outside world to come to a standstill for a couple of hours, is an empowering and significant sensation. The advantages of music being heard with silent focus and rapt attention are clear, but when Wagner initiated the idea that dimming the lights in the auditorium would encourage the most profound of personal experiences, and was happy that the public's identity could be subsumed so that only that of the music and its performers remained, he forged what can be a problematic gap between the audience and the music.

Many of the rituals of the modern concert experience reinforce that gap and support the idea that it is what happens on the stage that matters, not in the hall as a whole. But if we want to understand why live classical music is struggling to engage new audiences, we need to be aware of the subconscious signals we give and address as many as we feel able to change.

A hundred years ago there was no discernible difference between what the orchestra wore and what the audience wore. Most musicians wear full evening dress today because that is what the public used to wear to concerts too. But the fact that performers are now more smartly dressed than those listening gives the impression either that we haven't kept up with the society we play for or, worse, that we have no desire to do so. The suggestion that musicians are somehow self-serving and aloof is false of course, but it is folly to deny that this is how others can sometimes perceive us. Orchestras should look uniform and smart. A performance is indeed a special occasion. However, it needs to be one that is unquestionably for the audience's benefit. Conductors are free to choose their own clothes but balancing the desire to look contemporary without distancing yourself from the orchestra you want to feel part of attracts its fair share of fashion faux pas.

I once conducted a concert that was free for anyone who had never been to a concert before. Most of the people who phoned for tickets asked what they should wear. From within the profession, it is easy to underestimate the anxiety that many can feel when contemplating going to live classical music. Yet when I recall things I have been invited to that fall outside my natural comfort zone, I can empathise with those who wonder if there might be an unwritten code they need to adhere to. Most musicians don't care what an audience wears to concerts. We want people to be there in whatever outfit they enjoy wearing. But our wish to be part of the culture of our time would probably benefit from being more publicly articulated.

Although all audience members are responsible for their own level of engagement, it is up to the performers on the stage to encourage, enable, and maintain the listeners' intensity of attention. One of the reasons audiences sound as if they are concentrating more during concertos than during purely orchestral music is that a soloist, probably playing without music and usually facing the auditorium, is clearly playing to, and therefore for, the public. People will always respond more actively to someone who is perceived to be more actively interested in their response. But orchestras and conductors cannot visibly engage with the audience. Players have very complicated music to read, and a conductor to watch. The earliest conductors did in fact face the audience, but this might be considered a dubious choice today. Conductors, seemingly by definition, have their backs turned towards the public. The communication cannot be visual – and this is a problem in a world that sets so much store by what it sees.

A young and relative newcomer to classical concerts told me recently that she didn't know where to look during the performance. It was a sincere and valid question and for me to have reminded her that the word 'audience' derives from the Latin verb 'to hear' would have been to deny that much has changed since the word originated. Nor would it have helped for me to say it doesn't matter where she looked. To some people, it does. We live in a visual world.

Should music offer an alternative to that reality or embrace it? A performance that relies on the music alone is possible, but it might not be enough to justify the interest of a new generation for whom such a large number of other live experiences are available. The view that only the music matters might be a worthy ideal, but if it alienates more people than it attracts, it risks compromising the human connection that is its very purpose. We cannot afford to appear to be in denial of our audience. The event has to be as exciting as the music itself.

*

Whether or not conductors believe it is part of the job specifically to help in audience engagement, there is no denying the fact that we are in a position to do so. In some cases, it could even be the name and reputation of the conductor that has given someone the trust or curiosity to attend in the first place. Conductors are the ones whose entrance marks the formal start of the performance, who most visibly express the music, and who are viewed as the channel through which audiences offer their final applause. Rightly or wrongly, it is through us that orchestral music is *seen* to speak. Yet though a conductor's visual impact on the audience cannot be denied, it is a pity if a physical impression upstages the audible one. It is easy for a conductor's gestures to be more of a distraction than an aid, and there are plenty in an auditorium who seek to avoid looking at the conductor, however meaningful the physicality might be. Ideally the gestures are a frame for the musical picture, one that encourages focus and increases definition, proportional and supportive in character, but anonymously so, with an essential quality that would be fully appreciated only were it not to be there.

The pressure to have a public personality does not sit comfortably on every conductor's shoulders. Those that have that kind of confidence can use it to help give a more personal identity and contemporary relevance to what is essentially an abstract and timeless form of expression. Yet however charismatic a stage presence, or whatever illuminating and personable words are used to introduce the music from the stage, it is while the music is being played that the connection really matters. Everything else is just gift-wrapping. In the end, it's the quality of the musical commitment of every performer on the stage that sustains an audience's engagement in the experience.

A longing to perform is unlikely to have been the prime factor that motivated a classical musician in the first place. The majority of us didn't start learning an instrument because we wanted an audience. The original impulse is rarely about sharing music with others. Apart from anything else, you have to begin far too young for this aspect of your character to be fully realised. Talent and discipline are clearer pathways into the profession than a particularly outgoing personality. Whereas someone might want to be a rock musician because of the relationship with an audience that it affords them, a young classical musician's interest is more likely to be focused on a relationship with the music, the complexity of which demands such intense concentration that there is little time or space to engage with the audience at the same time. There are exceptions, but most classical musicians go into music first and performance second, while in rock music it is the other way around. To watch a rock concert is to be aware of extraordinary extra-musical efforts affecting the nature of its performance. Whatever you think about the music, you cannot help but be impressed by the commitment to sharing it.

I do not know how many people cough at rock concerts. But in my experience the theatre doesn't attract as many bronchitis sufferers as the concert hall. Is it the absence of visual variety that creates a restlessness or does the lack of an orchestra's individual identity mean that people don't consider it rude to 'interrupt'? Perhaps audiences are just more relaxed when they go to plays and feel less need to fidget as a result. Does even the very suggestion that there might be some kind of concert etiquette create an unnecessarily stressful environment in the first place?

Although there are anechoic chambers that offer an opportunity to experience the rare privilege of an almost complete absence of sound, in everyday life there is no such thing as silence. If there was, there might be more than one word for it. Even the proverbial pin drop is always accompanied by an ambient noise of one kind or another. Distant traffic, ticking seconds, singing birds, even, at times, one's own breath. Put two thousand people in a concert hall and the possibilities for true silence are pretty non-existent. But one of the things I love about so-called silence in music is that the audience and the players become as one in their contributions to the performance. Whether short or long, silence unites everyone in the hall, suspended in a pregnant limbo in which reflection on what was just heard blends imperceptibly with anticipation of what might come next. Silence is not a moment of emptiness, but a place that encompasses a countless number of thoughts and emotions.

It is significant how often composers put an indeterminate pause over a silence. They recognise they are not in a position to prescribe its exact length without knowing what the atmosphere is going to be like in the hall. A restless and distracted public offers a completely different experience from that emanating from a totally engaged audience. And though the music's needs do not change, the concentration level in the listeners has to have a bearing on how long the silences are held.

There is a theory that silence makes some people nervous, disquieted even, because they associate it with death, and that the challenge of confronting this connection is what leads to such anxious throat-clearing. Certainly, if you believe in eternal nothingness, it's going to be pretty quiet when you get there, and perhaps that's why both Shostakovich and Mahler composed so much significant emptiness into their final, valedictory symphonies. The intensity of these pieces exists more in the holes between the notes than in the notes themselves. Sound describes the specific, but silence expresses the infinite. 'Speech is silver. Silence is golden.'

If a silence is truly heard, it wields enormous power. For only in relation to silence can sound have meaning. I have had many concerts spoilt by a noisy audience. And the most memorable performances I have been part of are those in which complete stillness in the auditorium made an enormous contribution. But blaming the audience might be putting the cart before the horse. All in all, I feel we get the attention we deserve, and I suspect that the best concerts create the right atmosphere, rather than the other way around. From even before we raise our arms, conductors can invite a tone that sets the scene for the nature of the experience everyone is about to have. It isn't something you can be too self-conscious about – an audience would see through that – but a virtuous circle needs to start somewhere. It cannot happen in the hall if it has not begun on the stage.

★

The disappointment of a restless audience is not that it spoils my own enjoyment of what I am conducting, but that it means that there are clearly some who have lost interest in the music being played. What makes it more disappointing, though, is that you know that their loss of attention has an impact on the involvement of everybody else in the audience too. A concert is a communal event, and the connections that a great performance weave through all who hear it are its most valued purpose. That everyone is responsible for those connections is what makes it so special when it happens. But how to impress that responsibility on an audience without making it seem as if the experience has to be stiflingly formal is a question that is not easy to solve.

In most hunter-gatherer societies, music occurs within a social context and it is a relatively recent phenomenon that we are able to experience it on our own. Music is a catalyst for a connection between all who hear it. There is an energy in a concert hall or opera house that everyone breathes in. This breath is shared, and its air sustained long after the music's final strains have died away. The power of music lies not in the communication between the composer and the listener but between all who have ever experienced it, across continents of space and through generations of time. It is more than a medium through which composers and performers simply share their own experiences. The combination of feeling touched as an individual yet at the same time being made to feel part of something bigger has a spiritual consequence. Music can be unbearably moving to listen to yet consoling at the same time because you sense that your experience is profoundly human and universally shared. Every man is an island. Music offers easy and trustworthy bridges to cross.

A sense of community depends a lot on the space itself. In fact, 'space' was one of the more surprising answers given when audiences were asked by an orchestra's marketing department for the reasons they go to a concert. It is a word that sums up perfectly both the defined and the unlimited experience of a performance.

I have been lucky to perform in many of the world's most celebrated concert halls. But I have conducted in plenty of theatres, convention centres, and sports halls too. Even in a skateboard park. Despite the thrill that you get from performing in famous buildings such as the Royal Albert Hall or the Sydney Opera House, the inspiration you feel from the history of halls such as the Concertgebouw in Amsterdam or Vienna's Musikverein, the beauty of La Scala, Milan, or the acoustics of Suntory Hall in Tokyo, in my experience at least there has never been a direct correlation between the venue and the quality of the performance. As long as a building can shut out external sounds, a sense of containment can liberate the mind from the practicalities of life and allow it to engage in profound and thought-provoking experiences in all sorts of settings. Tradition is motivating; aesthetics are inspiring; and good acoustics are empowering, but something special can happen anywhere. A memorable concert is the result of far more than its visual or aural reality. It doesn't even need to be a technically perfect performance to create the intangible recognition that an exceptional quality of human expression is concentrating the widest range of thoughts and emotions into the smallest point of the here and now. There is no past, no future, no there, no anywhere. In that sense music is an expression of love, of absolute, timeless unity. It can succeed in the most unlikely of places.

Music is an emotional odyssey that can stretch the boundaries of our inner world and lift us out of that confined space and onto a plane of much greater proportions. It is rather like going to a religious ceremony. Though today's marketing departments might shudder at the thought of having their glamorous profession compared with that of the priesthood, one of classical music's strengths is the way it connects with spirituality rather than with reality. Both religious buildings and concert halls provide an opportunity to enter a closed space in order to discover an infinite one. Music is not a religion, but what links all artistic genius is its inexplicability and indefinability. It is not a coincidence that for those who believe in God, music is a way of trying to get closer to Him.

★

I wonder if the last bar of Beethoven's First Symphony has ever been heard in public. It contains only rests, but Beethoven wouldn't have written it if he did not want its silence to be in some sense experienced. The alacrity with which many in an audience start to clap often surprises me. Although genuinely motivated applause is always welcome, a piece is not necessarily over the instant the music stops.

There is a – literally – tacit understanding that most performances benefit from a brief period of silent preparation. The musical experience begins before the first notes are played. And for some, or perhaps many, time at the end is equally valid. Some music concludes with obvious invitations for reflection. Mahler's last three symphonies encourage lingering over their reluctant farewells, and only the most hard-hearted rush to interrupt these moments of profound introspection. Other works flag up their endings well in advance, but even then it can require time to digest their meaning fully. I always feel I have failed to do justice to the shock and horror of Shostakovich's Fifth Symphony if its brutally abrupt final bar is met with an immediate cheer.

Conductors can control when the experience starts, but are relatively powerless to influence when it ends. A gesture that delays an audience's response would probably need to be predetermined, and its artificiality could be somewhat self-defeating. Anyway, I'm not sure if performers are the best judges of when the intensity should be relaxed. Our concept of time can easily become skewed during the music, and we are unlikely to have the relevant objectivity to determine the validity of what we have just done. It's slightly embarrassing if, in some timeless, self-indulgent world, the musicians are more moved than those who have been listening.

Are the first to clap the most or the least affected by the performance? Might premature appreciation actually reveal a lack of appreciation? Or is it an overwhelming eagerness to be part of what has just happened? Maybe some musical experiences simply carry with them an irresistible need to express a reaction as soon as possible. Or is it just that knowing when a piece is over is something to publicise? I confess that, when performing, the adrenalin surge that accompanies a thrilling and upbeat finale is wonderfully fulfilled by immediate applause and if that applause is fractionally withheld, it's odd to have the fleeting sensation that everyone might have gone home. But many in an audience will feel no rush to respond, however special they thought the performance, and prefer to savour their reaction before sharing it publicly. Even if there is such a thing as a right time to clap, everyone has their own sense of when that should be, and there is no reason why those who want the applause delayed have any more rights than those who do not.

Appreciation is a fundamental part of human nature and clapping at musical performances is more than a simple sign of admiration and gratitude. It is a ritual with roots deep in the recesses of human consciousness, a physical gesture that connects every age and every culture. Whether heard as 'a ripple of' or 'thunderous', it is not surprising that the unique sound of applause is so often described in elemental terms.

Applause comes in a variety of forms. Some audiences like synchronisation. This starts out OK but can become awkward once people wonder what to do next – a dilemma that can be resolved by a kitsch synchronised acceleration. The Germans stamp their feet – if you passed the test. The Dutch give standing ovations every time, while in some countries what you think is a standing ovation turns out to be people making an early move for the exit. This prompted one conductor to remark that some audiences see only the back of him and he sees only the back of them. The most welcome applause is whatever sounds like a return to a basic childlike expression of unbridled spontaneous enthusiasm. We strive to avoid the predictable in performances and it is special when audiences respond with a similar absence of convention.

Unlike at the theatre, people clap at concerts before anything has happened, making a noise before the orchestra does and, more to the point, doing something together before the orchestra does. It is a ceremonial coming together that reflects a readiness on the part of the public. The community has been joined – a symbol that embraces the group dynamic. A baby's joy in 'pat-a-cake pat-a-cake' is an early consciousness of actively joining in with life, an interaction that I imagine creates a greater sense of belonging. That belonging is one of the things that makes a concert experience so powerful too.

In the often all too slender sliver of silence squashed up between the final notes of a piece and the start of the ensuing applause, musicians have to engage in a hasty transition from the role of player to that of purely performer. It is a journey that can be hard to achieve smoothly by those who find it a long way to travel. Of course, the whole concert has been a performance, but one that has happened through the cloak of the composer's music, and the nakedness of engaging with the audience without that shield can be psychologically hard. But receiving is a form of giving too and audiences want to know that their gratitude is welcomed. Taken to its extreme, humility can be perceived as a disregard for the public's opinion. An added complication for conductors is that we accept applause on behalf of everyone involved. Although most orchestras now turn to face the audience when they stand, it is still normally only the conductor who bows, and it isn't uncomplicated to seek to share the approbation without appearing overly self-deprecating. But those who can bow with modest yet sincere acceptance prolong the bond they have spent the last couple of hours trying to create. It's a pity to break the spell if you want the magic to last beyond the music's dying fall.

How musicians respond to applause is a more important part of performing than one might think. The Suzuki method of teaching the violin starts each lesson with a bow. Bowing comes before bowing. This might just sound charming, but to be able to accept applause with grace and gratitude, avoiding false modesty or hubris, is a requisite part of engaging with the audience, and for those for whom this might not come naturally, disregarding its significance can easily be misinterpreted. What arises out of shyness can come across as diffidence – especially to audiences who might be surprised to witness a performer's change in personality once the music has stopped. But it's perfectly possible to be uninhibited for as long as the music sounds, yet feel a need to retreat into a shell when it is over. The charisma that can express extremely private emotions within a musical context is not necessarily the same as one that can deal with the public reality of an audience.

★

Whatever the hall, whichever the orchestra, whoever the conductor, it is still the music that is the reason people come to concerts. Although some conductors have less control over programming than others, choosing which pieces to perform is our first responsibility to the public.

Audiences vary hugely in what they want to hear. Some want to listen only to pieces they know, others are interested only in something new. And those who want a balance between the two are unlikely to agree on where that balance lies. Trying to cater for a broad range of tastes without resorting to a low common denominator is challenging. Programme Weber and you risk denying the curious. Put Webern on the poster and the traditionalists won't attend. Combine the two and you risk putting everyone off.

Box-office figures prove the conservative nature of the majority of concertgoers. Given the proverbial 'he who pays the piper calls the tune', the temptation to accept this reality is understandable, but the benefits of doing so are short term. In the long run, there's a danger that by excessively repeating the most popular repertoire, the classical music industry is sowing the seeds of its own destruction. And exhausting the popular pieces can drain the commitment of the performers too. At that point, even the public's support for them will start to wane. Once these two things combine, the days of live concerts are numbered and to assume that the drawing power of the classical music world's most famous works cannot be affected by the quality with which these works are performed is insulting to both player and audience alike.

Having said that, repetition does seem to be part of the

reason behind a piece's popularity. Works such as Beethoven's Fifth Symphony, Mozart's Fortieth, or Rossini's *William Tell* Overture are all based on small, easily identifiable ideas heard over and over again. Cognitive scientists think that it is precisely this that appeals to us. Our ability to recognise patterns activates the pleasure-and-reward systems of the brain. However, recent studies suggest that our brains like being surprised by what we hear too. Philip Ball has pointed out that if we only ever had our expectations fulfilled we would prefer simple music all the time, and as plain sailing as the most famous works appear, their musical patterns are actually highly sophisticated and irregular. It is the subtle transformations that the greatest composers effect on their motifs that have allowed their works to stay so popular for so long.

Music needs to have a certain familiarity for most people to enjoy it. But just as composers balance the predictable with the unexpected, it is crucial that we do something similar when it comes to programming concerts. Limiting people's exposure to a variety of classical music limits the pleasure they receive from it. There are many more great works than there are popular ones and the 'world's most loved classical music' does not have to be a finite list. Lengthening that list is the only sustainable future and, given that most orchestra players are disproportionally disenfranchised from the process of choosing the music they play, the responsibility for doing this falls primarily to the conductor. Audiences can identify with an individual musician in a way that they cannot with a group of a hundred, and if the public knows and trusts the taste and judgement of the conductor, this strong personal connection opens up the possibility for far greater risk and adventure when it comes to planning the music that is played.

There is no point putting on a performance if no one comes to listen. As with the tree falling in the forest, if no one hears the music how can we be sure it exists? Audiences are the justification for what we do and the choice of repertoire must be one that sounds attractive, one that tells its own story or is part of a bigger one, and one in which the works contrast or complement each other in a way that shows they were not just thrown together by a committee. Audiences deserve more than a concerto the soloist likes, a symphony the conductor likes, and an overture that allows people who are late not to miss anything important.

A good programme should be the result of the relationship between the orchestra and its community – but making sure that this relationship is constantly evolving is up to the cultural institution itself. Although the public's tastes cannot be ignored, a situation in which ticket sales are the only arbiter of repertoire is not an artistic vision. Fortunately, wanting many people to come and listen is not the same as being motivated purely by the box office. There are undoubtedly organisations that prove a creative middle ground does exist. They offer a leadership that people want to follow, promoting a definite goal for the future, alongside an equally clear understanding of the reality of their here-and-now. It is possible to see the horizon at the same time as the bottom line and manage both without contradiction or compromise.

A desire to remain relevant is complicated by most programmes being chosen significantly ahead of the event.
For many concerts this is at least two years in advance,
for operas much longer than that. Although this is necessary for all sorts of practical reasons, it's not surprising that
by the time you get to the performance the accusation of
living in the past can be levelled against you. Musicians
change too. What might have once seemed a good idea can
be something you might not feel quite so committed to
when the time actually comes. The degree of forward planning involved militates against the spur of the moment.
Of course, there needs to be time to prepare the music
and publicise the performance but when a conductor's or
soloist's illness causes plans to be changed at the eleventh
hour, the welcome element of spontaneity feels all too rare.

A variety of guest conductors offers both an orchestra
and a community a wider range of styles than even the
most catholic of music directors can provide, but though
freelance conductors might know what music they want to
conduct, a discussion with the orchestra's artistic admin-
istrator to determine the relevance and appropriateness of
any particular choice is vital. Good artistic administrators
know all the local agendas involved, and the best have an
instinct about how to blend them together. Like cooking,
the ability to create the ideal programme is an art not a skill,
and sometimes the repertoire looks good on paper but for
whatever reason doesn't take flight when it matters. Magic is
not a box that can be ticked. When everything does work, it
can feel like luck, but it is notable that with the best artistic
administrators luck seems to strike more often.

I love planning programmes. It is an honour to be asked to use your imagination to create or influence what you hope will be a memorable experience for all involved. You try to be original without being alienating, fashion a narrative that isn't limiting, and design a combination of pieces that inspires the orchestra and audience to feel as if they are taking part in something unique. There is such a wealth of works to choose from, so many riches to play with, that concocting a journey that is both thought-provoking and rewarding is like playing with an endless treasure trove of possibilities.

Sometimes an orchestra proposes a particular programme in order to fit in with its season as a whole. Over time I have become more able to be accommodating to a greater number of requests, and the wish to be part of something bigger than my own experience is strong. But you have to love the pieces you perform and if you don't care deeply about a work it is hard to sustain the necessary concentration to study it, encourage the musicians to rehearse it, or share its passion with the public in performance. It is a knowledge, understanding, and love for the music that justifies your right to lead its advocacy and without those things it can be hard to have the confidence to take on that role.

I am always in awe of orchestra musicians when I think of the number of pieces they have played and compare their tally with the repertoire of even the most musically wide-ranging conductors. Add to that the extraordinary variety of genres and styles orchestras perform, and you realise how well rounded their exposure to music must be.

Players will have their preferences, but as they are expected to play everything from Albinoni to Zappa they can't afford to be prejudiced. Conductors rarely have to perform music they do not like. That is an amazing privilege, but it does limit the occasions on which you might be pleasantly surprised or challenged by working outside a natural habitat that you might have previously identified for yourself.

I have come to realise that I am not necessarily the best judge of what music I should conduct, and I am always appreciative of the thoughtful objectivity of others introducing me to a piece I would not have considered on my own. When that happens, the freshness to my enthusiasm is very stimulating and I suspect more persuasive too. There is no doubting the zeal of the recently converted.

Some conductors respond to a broad range of music and can do more than a professional job with many different styles. Others are more particular and enjoy limiting their repertoire in order to understand fewer pieces more deeply. But there is a point at which raising the stakes ever higher for a small list of works becomes an issue of vanity. It is dangerous if an intensity of care spills over into making the experience about you, and it can be suffocating to try to cope with the sort of self-imposed pressure that comes from wanting to conduct a piece better than you have ever conducted it before. There is something hubristic about believing that every concert should be an opportunity to lay your soul bare at the feet of the composer, and that there are only a few pieces that can justify the sacrifice of your humility for the greater good!

Music is about breadth as much as depth. Knowing the

intricate details of any piece is important, but to a certain extent it is also true that the more music you know overall the better. The understanding of any one Beethoven symphony is likely to be helped by having conducted them all. There is a point at which quantity of knowledge inhibits its quality but where that sliding scale rests is different for everyone, and is constantly changing for everyone too. Finding the balance between Jack-of-All-Symphonies and Master-of-Some is a lifelong search.

*

Getting the repertoire choices right is crucial. We should respect the past and those who want to continue to enjoy it. But if we don't introduce audiences to the music of today, our concerts will become a reflection of a society that places no value on the future. Those societies die. We have to find the balance that takes both the past and the future into consideration. The lure of the familiar will always be stronger than any attraction to something unknown, and though alienating many with a constant shock of the new would bankrupt most orchestras within a year, a reliance on predictable programming will bankrupt them culturally in not much more time than that.

People's resistance to new music is intriguing. And not only to new music. There are pieces that are a hundred years old that one still hesitates to programme. Were the likes of Schoenberg and Webern so far ahead of their time, or is it a sign of our own times that we have ceased to want to explore the full potential of our experience? Is there a feeling that we have discovered all we need to know? Or are we too scared to turn inwards for the explorations that still remain? There is certainly more audience curiosity when it comes to contemporary art, literature, drama, or dance. The reluctance of so many music lovers to be daring in their choice of music is an acknowledgement that music is a language that many are fearful of not understanding. But whenever people tell me they don't understand modern music, I wonder if I 'understand' any music at all. I'm not sure that is the part of our brain we are meant to be using. Understanding is a form of limitation, and music is nothing if not unlimited. It communicates subliminally and audiences should feel empowered to make their own mind up about something they hear on a less cerebral basis. If the profession is too scared to programme new pieces too often, it only serves to highlight the public perception that they are a challenge. New music needs to be normalised to prevent it fulfilling the stereotype it so often attracts. It is not a coincidence that the orchestras that perform the most of it are the ones doing so most successfully. They are not responding to a need in their particular community; they are creating that need in the first place. Although a fear of alienating an established demographic is fair enough, the regular absence of contemporary music risks putting new audiences off just as much. It reinforces the popular belief that classical music is about the past and therefore for the past. You get the audiences you deserve, and though some marketing experts might prefer to promote the already promoted, fortune favours the bold.

Of course, it would be disingenuous to suggest that

playing modern music is always a pleasure and it can be frustrating not to benefit from the process of natural selection that occurs over time. But the future depends more on the present than the past. And we are in a position to control the present, even if it is tempting to tell ourselves we cannot. Our reaction to the new is inevitably different from our reaction to something we know. Contemporary art is a reflection of its time and looking into a mirror can sometimes be an uncomfortable experience. But music of our time both stimulates and sustains our curiosity, an inquisitiveness that is central to who we are as a species. It would be a poorer world if we valued only what we liked.

Going to a concert is inevitably an abdication of a certain degree of control. At an art gallery you decide how long you stand in front of any picture. There is no obligation to finish a book you do not like. If you go to a party, you are happy to meet old friends, and perhaps hopeful of making some new ones, but you feel relatively secure in your ability to walk away from any situation you are not enjoying. This degree of self-determination is not available to the concert-goer, expected to sit in the dark, not only figuratively perhaps, isolated from anyone else's opinions until it is over. There are not many ways round the established process of musical performance but it might not be the most conducive format in which to experience the unknown.

★

Most classical music lovers agree which pieces of music are great or not. Despite a wide range of personal preferences, there's a general consensus as to what these masterpieces are. But when it comes to judging performances, there is rarely unanimity. This subjective receptivity suggests that a significant contribution to the experience is the audience itself. And though the musician's contribution might be definable, the more mysterious component that a public brings is equally important.

A lot depends on the level of an audience's anticipation and how this then compares with the reality of what it experiences. In much of the arts world anticipation is based on reputation. But if there's a disconnect between your enjoyment and what you have been led to expect, it is possible to doubt your own reaction to the event before you question the validity of its promotional hype. If marketing leads the product, rather than the other way around, the risk is that this divests the public of its right to trust its own opinion. In turn, this only serves to distance its engagement. Publicising a performance is almost as important as the performance itself, but if it is not done with knowledge of its subject and a respect for its audience it won't ever be an investment in the long-term interests of the musical organisation. If you believe the best way to sell a Jaguar is to pretend it is a Ferrari, you are not going to get much return business.

People on the business wing of the profession have much to gain from encouraging musical hierarchies. Profit and loss is easier to identify within the framework of a pyramid. But though the repute of individual musicians can easily and quickly change, it is far harder for orchestras to alter the classification that they have been assigned by the music industry. Our culture is obsessively competitive. Artistic competition is an idle sport. Orchestras should not be judged on which have the highest-paid players, the most valuable instruments, or the oldest traditions. The question is rather which ones transcend these realities and give magical performances the like of which could not be surpassed. Obviously, some orchestras do this more often than others, but there isn't one that is incapable of having a bad night. Musicians are human after all. I would guess there are hundreds of ensembles that, with the right combination of favourable conditions, can offer a truly sensational experience. The potential to be, on any given night, 'the greatest orchestra in the world' is widespread, an achievement that I believe is reached more often than people might think. Few musicians are susceptible to the hype of their profession, and they know the reality of what they do. But a public perception that is allowed to undervalue a particular orchestra's quality risks creating audiences that are less happy to trust their own opinions. It is a shame if, away from the more established musical capitals of the world, a mistaken cultural insecurity doubts the brilliance with which many less famous orchestras play.

★

A conductor's relationship with those in the audience is complex. We are the individuals they most seek to relate to, yet we never look at them while we are conducting. We accept their applause despite not making a single sound. We are conscious that a public identity will help sell more tickets but know that if our persona upstages the music those listening will be the first to be disappointed. These inhibitions can lead to a denial of public responsibility, which then limits the opportunities for work in the future. Like many other contradictions inherent in the job, how we handle these internal conflicts defines a lot of our professional success. It also contributes a great deal to personal happiness. They are not necessarily the same thing.

6

Conducting Yourself

'There's this world,' she banged the wall graphically,
'and there's this world,' she thumped her chest. 'If you want to
make sense of either, you have to take notice of both.'
Jeanette Winterson, *Oranges Are Not the Only Fruit*

An internet search for jokes about conductors comes up with 436,000 results. That's almost twice as many as there are about viola players. But whereas the latter are mainly patronising and even slightly affectionate in tone, the humour surrounding the conducting profession is positively vitriolic:

What do great conductors have in common?
They are all dead.

What do you need when you have a conductor up to his neck in quicksand?
More quicksand.

What's the difference between a conductor and a sack of manure?
The sack.

Why are conductors' hearts coveted for transplants?
They've had so little use.

Those are a few of the more printable ones.

There are several obvious reasons musicians are rude about conductors, and probably plenty more that I don't know about. But the internal disdain is so pervasive that there must be more to it than the fairly normal frustrations many people have with those in positions of authority.

Players practise for a long time in order to earn not much money working very hard, and there is an understandable irritation that a profession that often pays its orchestras so badly should remunerate its conductors so well. Conductors have worked hard since an early age too, but they are unlikely to have been studying conducting all that time. Despite spending less time learning our craft, however, the job leapfrogs us into a position where we have far more musical autonomy than instrumentalists do. Orchestra musicians have little say over what they play, or when, or where, or how they play it. In something as personal as music a lack of self-determination can be deeply problematic. Music is a means of expressing yourself, and always having to do so on someone else's terms can easily build up a tension that needs to find its release somewhere. Conductors are an easy target, whether they are directly responsible for the problem or not.

Historically speaking, the conductor is a recent arrival on the musical scene. Barely a hundred years have passed since conducting became a profession in its own right. To swan in late is one thing. To proceed to tell people what to do, and to receive plentiful public approbation for doing so, can easily generate aggravation if the players don't consider the conductor worthy of the authority the role can provide.

Some believe that conducting should never be anyone's sole profession and that only by being a composer or an instrumentalist as well can you develop and maintain a deep connection to music. The argument is that if they are separated from the reality of making a sound, conductors are alienated from the players in a way that can easily lead to suspicion. To paraphrase the West Indian cricket writer and historian C. L. R. James: What do they know of conducting who only conducting know? Certainly, professional musicians who have decided to turn their hand to conducting later in life, even if they are physically or even psychologically less capable, receive a degree of trust and respect from an orchestra because of what they have already achieved musically on their own. Initially, at least.

Despite 'just' conducting being viewed by some as overly specialised, most conductors are categorised even further when it comes to their musical strengths and weaknesses. There is scepticism that someone might conduct Bach as successfully as they do Ligeti, or a feeling that if you like *Swan Lake* you are not cut out for Mahler's Ninth Symphony. An all-rounder is often considered lacking in specific excellence. I suspect that at any particular time most conductors are better at one style than another and that our temperament needs to in some way coincide with that of the composer, but our personalities are constantly evolving, just like everyone else's, and it's a shame if musical pigeonholes deny us the broad approach we can often be criticised for not having.

Conversely, there are a huge number of extra-musical boxes that modern conductors are expected to tick. Many spend a great deal of time persuading people of the value of philanthropy; engage in the huge responsibility of hiring new players, and the far more soul-searching one of explaining why it might be time for someone to step down; and reach out to those in the community who for whatever reason don't consider classical music to be something for them. And if you are good at all these things, there will inevitably be some who don't think you understand the music of Brahms!

The ideal conductor has musical, physical, and psychological skills, yet because other people actually play the music, it's possible to be deficient in any one of these areas and to a certain extent still get results. Take two of these three attributes away and the players will continue to cover the shortfalls. Be devoid of all three and what remains is just your self-confidence. Confidence gets you a long way in conducting. Even some prime ministers have thought they could have a go. But though believing you can do the job might enable you to do so, it does not necessarily mean you will do it very well. Ironically it is an orchestra's skill that enables a wide range of conducting ability and it is the frequency with which players have to cover up a conductor's weaknesses that probably lies behind some of their resentment. A musician's instinct, not to say pride, is to make the best of any situation and, as professionals, orchestra musicians know it's their job to do just that. Most consider their responsibility to the audience to be more important than their opinion of the conductor and they know that it is in their interest for the concert to be as good as possible, even if in making it so they perpetuate the success of an individual they don't rate highly. They keep their frustration off the stage – a public lip, well and truly bitten.

The potential for discontent is not purely musical, and some conductors wield a considerable amount of personal and political power. But in the main that abusive relationship is a historical stereotype and it is much less likely at the highest level of the profession than it used to be – and certainly not wherever players have been given a significant say in who conducts them. The relationship is evolving, and conductors know that to be rude and condescending doesn't make them appear better musicians. Nor does it make better music. Even so, it is going to take a long time before the jokes sound out of date.

It could be worse. There are 16 million online results for jokes about lawyers. But misgivings about the legal profession are generally well known, and one of the dichotomies within classical music is that the professional insider's view of conductors is at such odds with how the public perceives us. The contradiction is a strange one to live with. It is not straightforward to work at the centre of such divergent images, when the truth, like most truths, is far more interesting and varied than these two extremes suggest.

The dynamic between orchestra and conductor might not be helped by the fact that the players never express any disappointment directly. Well, almost never. There is an etiquette of professional civility as well as just basic human politeness that shields a conductor from the specifics of an orchestra's opinion. But a stony silence doesn't necessarily camouflage what the players are thinking. You can see it in their eyes and, perhaps even more easily, hear it in their playing.

There are plenty of orchestra musicians who on an individual level are friendly to and overtly appreciative of many conductors. There are others who don't want any personal relationship whatsoever. The use of the title 'maestro' is partly a form of faux respect designed precisely to allow players to keep their distance. It is an antiquated term but when I ask people not to use it, many seem rather at a loss for an alternative. Plenty would prefer not to use my actual name, either because they don't feel they know me well enough for 'Mark', do not quite trust themselves to pronounce 'Wigglesworth', or most likely would prefer to remain personally disengaged from someone they see as their boss on that particular day. I remember once asking an orchestra not to call me 'maestro', only for a player immediately, and pointedly, to do just that. It was clear that that individual not only thought that I had no right to tell him what to call me but also that he had no wish to identify me as a real person and would rather keep his distance in whatever way he could.

An uncertainty of nomenclature works the other way around too, and it can be difficult for conductors to decide how best to address individual players in the orchestra. If you know them well, anything other than first-name terms seems unnecessarily formal. If you don't know them at all, the only alternative to calling musicians by the name of the instrument they play is to learn their individual names in advance. This is not a particularly hard thing to do, but it can come across as an affectation – especially as the relaxed nature of modern society complicates your choice of whether a first name or a surname is more appropriate.

And if you know some of the players but not others you have to choose whether you are going to be natural and therefore inconsistent, or egalitarian and therefore occasionally slightly awkward. Some players prefer not to have their personal identity attached to any comment the conductor might make. Others cannot understand why they are not being treated like a human being. It's often a no-win situation, though praising the individual and criticising the instrument is usually a fairly successful compromise.

There is an advantage to keeping a distance. Many players would prefer too cold a relationship to too personal a one and perhaps their collective disregard for conductors is a coping mechanism for what in many cases is still a very one-sided relationship. It comes with the territory and need not be something conductors should take personally. Unpopularity can be the price you pay for the privilege of leadership; as Tony Blair termed it, 'the cost of conviction'. He should know.

However, just developing a thick skin is not the answer. Einstein thought that seeing yourself as separate from the universe was a delusional prison. It might be that some conductors find it safer that way but any barriers you erect inevitably function in both directions. You have to be sensitive to others' needs even if oblivious to your own. Empathy takes a certain amount of courage, and to be able to express your musical feelings without letting anyone else's negativity upset you is not easy. There's nothing wrong with appearing vulnerable, though. It can be a very persuasive trait. But you need an inner resilience to remain focused on the music and your desire to conduct it.

Conductors have to remember that if they feel they are being met with apathy and cynicism, these forces are not necessarily representative of the whole orchestra. A negative minority can easily appear more powerful than a positive majority and you try to make sure you conduct for those who care the most, even if human nature often determines that that energy is less conspicuously expressed. Ultimately you hope to earn the respect of as many players as possible. That is far more important for an orchestra that sees its relationship with the conductor as a means to an end, not an end in itself.

Respect comes from your qualities as a musician but it also depends on your willingness to accept the difficult as well as the easy parts of the job. Good performances rarely happen on their own. Often the harder of two options needs to be chosen and in an orchestral context that decision is normally the responsibility of the conductor. On an individual basis, working hard is something players have never shied away from. They could not have got a job in the first place without pushing themselves over many years. But with a large group of people, the temptation to avoid a more challenging path is strong, and though they might not admit it among their peers, players look to the conductor to insist on achieving the highest possible standards. As long as musicians feel the rehearsals are making the performance better they will respect the one who persists in making that happen. They might not admit it out loud. They might even grumble. But I think deep down they are grateful and glad of the opportunity to do their best.

★

A conductor's opportunity to be a musician is to a certain extent dependent on what players think of our work. How an audience judges our performance is connected to how an orchestra judges us too. That makes our position unique within the music profession. Yet a performance is about more than our relationship with the musicians. It is not a popularity competition.

I once asked some players to write down what they looked for in a conductor. Their collated response revealed a daunting job description:

> Conductors need good baton technique, rehearsal
> technique, musicianship, knowledge, interpretative
> conviction, an ability to communicate, to stretch and
> challenge people, to make the performance better than
> the rehearsals, to be inspirational, have a good ear, clear
> thoughts, reliability, competence, rhythm, an expressive
> face, sense of structure, ability to accompany, style,
> suitability for the repertoire, originality, knowledge
> of string bowing, an ability to collaborate, analyse
> and solve difficulties, explain why things need to be
> repeated, empower people, train people, make people
> listen. They must not talk, over-rehearse, under-
> rehearse, or be musically detached. They must have
> good manners, humour, respect, approachability,
> enthusiasm, encouragement, humility, positive spirit,
> patience, leadership, sincerity, audibility, creativity,
> an awareness of everyone, self-control, and strength

of character. They must be relaxed, self-confident, empathetic, punctual, motivating, polite, authoritative, realistic, interesting, charismatic, persevering, committed, well dressed, and even-tempered. They must be popular with audiences, and show chastity, poverty, and obedience to the score. They must not be egocentric, intimidating, sarcastic, rude, boring, nervous, bullying, ugly, smelly, over-familiar, detached, pedantic, cynical, insecure, or blinkered. They must not change things for the sake of it, glare at mistakes, or hit the stand.

I am glad I have never hit the stand.

It is impossible to please an entire orchestra. If you are one of the conductors who makes music in order to connect with people as opposed to one who works with people in order to make music, you are going to find that reality difficult to accept. Train companies have started to call their conductors 'onboard supervisors', and while some orchestra musicians might prefer that to be the limit of our role, others see this as the bare minimum. You just have to carry out the job as you believe it should be done and hope the percentages work in your favour. However many people are bored or galvanised by what we do, the only thing we can really control is the desire to be ourselves. Or at least to be true to ourselves – which is not quite the same thing. To be ourselves would be to express the multitude of contradictions that make up every human being and these characteristics need to be both simplified and magnified if they are to offer clear and inspirational leadership to others. That modification will vary depending on the particular situation, but I don't think it should ever stray from your own inner truth. I believe that to be disingenuous is perhaps the only unforgivable failing, as it carries with it the suggestion that players are not intelligent enough to see through it.

Conductors connect in one way or another with a large number of people within the profession and success depends on an ability to be part of a complex web of relationships with a wide variety of colleagues: administrators, agents, audiences, choreographers, chorus masters, composers, critics, dancers, designers, directors, librarians, librettists, managers, musical assistants, orchestras, promoters, publicists, publishers, recording producers, singers, soloists, sound engineers, and stage managers. I have alphabetised them not just to be politically correct but because at any specific moment our relationship with any one of them is the most important relationship we have. Yet, despite the fact that conductors do not exist in a vacuum, and that we cannot achieve anything without collaborating with others, the profession is a solitary one. It is the relationship you have with yourself that is the one that defines your interpretation of the ones you have with others.

Conductors are judged all the time. By players, audiences, critics, other conductors, and the music profession in its widest sense. Everyone feels entitled to an opinion on those who put their heads above the parapet. And so they should. Conductors do not expect any less, and we would probably be slightly troubled without it. But, despite all the good and bad that comes our way, the most significant criticisms are the ones we give ourselves. You always know if you have prepared a piece well, rehearsed it appropriately, given a good performance, and although being open to external advice can be incredibly helpful, if you are being truly honest with yourself, your own view is the only one that you can guarantee carries with it no agenda or bias. Even your closest and most supportive friends are going to be affected by the relationship they have with you. It is impossible for them not to be. Unconditional personal support is an invaluable thing that every performer needs to come home to, but that is not quite the same thing as the artistic truth that comes from uncompromising self-analysis.

Conductors are not the only people who need to be able to distinguish between their professional and personal achievements and failures, and there are many jobs that reflect who you are rather than what you do. To lead such an interconnected life is fortunate, but you have to try to maintain an equilibrium between your work's highs and lows and find concord in their contradictions if you are to remain good company for your friends and family. Without wanting to get too 'Oprah-tic' about it all, you have to like yourself, irrespective of what other people think of you.

*

In a fanciful sense conductors are never alone. We spend our whole working life engaging in the thoughts of others. It's a rather pretentious thing to say but it is impossible to feel lonely with a score in front of you, even though most of the time the person 'talking' to you is dead. Preparing a piece also develops some form of a bond with everyone who has conducted the work before you. You know they must have asked the same questions of the music, come up with comparable answers, and experienced similar labour pains as you all aim to forge your own connection to the work in hand. Conductors do not talk to each other much. We have little need for a collective noun. That's partly because there is normally only one of us in a room at any given time, but a degree of insecurity plays its part too. And though there are many similarities to the problems we all face, the right solution for one is often not the best choice for another. Most conductors are more than happy to pass on to others their experiences of an orchestra or a piece. But as interesting or comforting as those experiences might be, they are normally so particular to the conductor concerned that whether they have any real relevance to anyone else is debatable.

For me, studying scores is the most exhausting part of the job. Being open to every possibility, investigating every avenue, asking every question, and considering every solution is extremely time-consuming. But, for me at least, exploring all the possibilities in advance is what makes it easier to persuade others of the value of the specific choices I want them to make. I also find the intensity of focus necessary to process the printed page into imaginary sound very demanding. There is a point at which taking in more information simply pops my brain balloon, but the main tension of this limit comes from it being impossible ever to say you really know a piece.

Understanding that every great work is ultimately un-scalable can be intimidating. But it can be inspiring too.

There is nothing wrong with feeling inadequate in the face of a masterpiece. What you don't want is to feel inadequate in front of a hundred musicians, and it is tempting to believe that the confidence you need to be able to conduct can be gained from an understanding of the music you are conducting. But if that is the purpose of your study, your knowledge will just be a security blanket with which you risk smothering your own as well as the orchestra's musical fire. Although knowledge of the score is vital, relying on it solely, to protect yourself with it even, is never going to result in a great performance.

Studying the music is a good starting point, the only starting point, but it is purely the beginning of the preparation process. As a goal in itself, it's actually a sort of vanity – a self-consciousness that takes you further away from the very thing you are trying to get closer to. To resist accepting the invisibility of a masterpiece's horizons can become an obsession. The danger of knowing too much is that it can limit your openness to the musical opinions of the orchestra musicians: an unconcealed certainty in what you want to hear can be perceived by players as devaluing their own contributions. Your knowledge needs to inspire confidence but should not be so visibly sure of itself that it results in an arrogant squashing of a sense of shared responsibility. Your preparation should be like the roots of a tree: essential but invisible.

Too much predetermination can inhibit your own spontaneous creativity too. The performance becomes purely a recreation of your preconceptions and, however well thought through they might be, a denial of the possibility for the unexpected strangles the life out of your own musicianship as well as that of the players. It can also just become confusing. Heisenberg's uncertainty principle – 'the closer you approach an object, the more you submit it to distortions' – is a valid pitfall when it comes to musical study. It is understandable to fear chaos, but if your home is too immaculate it simply doesn't feel lived in. In some ways learning a score is the easy bit. It is forgetting what you have learned that takes courage. Both parts of the process are equally important and both are a skill in their own right. You try to trust that something forgotten is not something never known.

When I started to conduct professionally, a very sage musician gave me a copy of *The Wisdom of Insecurity* by Alan Watts. I read it at the time but it took me at least twenty years to take the hint. As crucial as studying a score is, if the confidence you gain from doing so is more an emotional crutch than a musical guide it is not going to be especially helpful to the orchestra. 'Don't suck for comfort the finger that points the way,' Watts says. To imagine there is such a thing as musical security is to fail before you start to try. As disconcerting as freedom is, security is an illusion, and you have to let yourself be vulnerable, both to the music and the situation. From this openness springs the source of the most special performances of all.

According to Zen masters, the only way to hit the target is not to aim. Of course, Zen masters are rarely faced with scores by Stockhausen and I'm not sure how philosophically orchestras would respond to a conductor using that as an excuse for being unprepared. Music is not served well by conductors breezing through. But overthinking things doesn't work either. Sometimes in order to feel safe we just create tensions, and it is worth remembering that thought can inhibit creativity as much as stimulate it. Pasternak felt that asking too many questions simply makes you old before your time. Maybe is all we have.

★

Balancing an uncertainty necessary to ask the right questions with the confidence to believe in the answers you find is important for all creative artists, especially performing ones. How do we maintain sufficient curiosity to continue to improve in what we do, while at the same time enjoying the necessary conviction to convince others of our conclusions? As the Chinese proverb aptly puts it, 'He who strides cannot walk. He who tiptoes cannot stand.'

Searching for the truth of a piece of music is an admirable goal. But that truth, or at least our own understanding of that truth, is constantly changing. I have often embarrassed myself with how convinced I am that my previous thoughts were wrong because I know I would have been absolutely certain of them at the time. Luckily it is not a contradiction to believe that there is only one possible interpretation yet also to know that that interpretation will be different the next time you play the piece. In fact, this is the ideal combination as it offers the best chances of success and the most likely possibility of improvement.

It is the artist's lot, even perhaps a duty, to be unsatisfied. This isn't as bleak as it sounds. It is a privilege to be on a journey that never ends, that constantly asks unanswerable questions, and musicians are lucky to always have a reason to make the next performance better. But the absence of a finishing line can be confronting for anyone with a perfectionist streak.

There is nothing wrong with wanting the best but, as a motivation in itself, perfectionism kills the joy of music. It is a barrier to self-expression, and an unattainable goal. There can never be a perfect performance and even if you thought you had succeeded, others would disagree. Only by giving up on perfection's attainability can you start to get closer to it, and only by accepting little mistakes can you prevent yourself from being the victim of a larger one. The vast majority of errors I make are the result of trying not to make different ones. My defence for something I did is that I was trying not to do something else. But negative motivation never works. Trying to eradicate the mistakes that marred your previous attempts is a backward-looking position that prevents you seeing where you are going. Of course, we have to learn from our past, but that process should not interfere with the reality of the present, and if we insist on seeing everything with absolute clarity before we decide, we shall never make a decision. The happiest performers are those who see an endless journey as a pleasure, an inspiration in itself. They belong to the 'better to travel than to arrive' brigade, and know that beating oneself up about falling short is more about vanity than creativity. It is better to be happy than to be perfect.

★

There are a variety of ways young conductors get their first chance to stand in front of a professional orchestra. For me it was the exposure that came from a competition. Some get their break on the recommendation of other conductors, and there are some who have made a name for themselves as musicians in other ways. A few decide to form their own orchestra rather than to sit around waiting to be invited to conduct an already established one. An opera house still offers a relatively measured approach to the podium in that there are various roles within a theatre that need to be done by a team of conductors, but it would be a bit of a stretch to call this a career ladder. Plenty perceived to be on it would point out how many rungs were missing. Although a production's need for assistant conductors, offstage conductors, chorus conductors and the like offers an opportunity for progression with a safety net that comes from being part of a company, this is a route whose validity is increasingly ignored. Whatever path has presented itself, orchestras make their mind up about their conductor based solely on what they see in front of them. They will accept any backstory if they consider you deserving of the responsibility entrusted to you.

It is hard to judge whether a conductor is ready for a professional situation. You probably do not even know yourself. It is such a specific relationship that there is no way to prepare for it. The well-known joke about someone in New York asking, 'How do I get to Carnegie Hall?' and getting the answer 'Practise!' cannot apply to conductors. There are no professional practice scenarios. There are only deep ends, and though there are varying levels of pressure within the profession, every orchestra has a number of minimum expectations.

I cannot imagine a situation in which someone's very first experience of conducting would be with a professional orchestra. As a student, you will have conducted your peers, probably amateur orchestras as well, and will be well versed in the physical and practical parts of the job. But nothing can prepare you for the psychological make-up of a large body of professional people. You try to deny how daunting this is by telling yourself to focus on your relationship with the composer, hoping to ignore the pressure that's exerted by so much knowledge and ability sitting in front of you. But who in their right mind disregards such a depth of experience? How do you differentiate between the influences that are going to help and those that will inhibit you? You can't take them all on board. But to take no notice of any is a missed opportunity to improve.

When I was young I remember someone telling me after a concert that I was conducting the wrong orchestra. It was not that he didn't feel I was good enough but that he thought young conductors needed a particular type of attitude from an orchestra to feel relaxed enough to do their best. There are plenty of stories of orchestras giving a conductor a hard time, and most of us remember the bruises. They were probably well deserved, but if the friction turns into a curbing of musicianship then nobody wins – not the conductor, not the orchestra, and certainly not the music itself. Nevertheless, as unsettling as any tension is (for everybody involved), there's nothing worse for a conductor than an orchestra that is apathetic. On the whole, I welcome it when players vent their frustrations. It shows how much they care; it brings an issue out into the open, and I get a chance either to defend my choices or to make alternative ones. But there is very little you can do to counteract the aggression of passive indifference. Nothing comes from nothing.

With the right orchestra, a young conductor's naivety can be infectious. Mike Brearley, at one time captain of the English cricket team, has written about the power of 'boyhood sources of energy and illusion'. The belief that something is easy is one of the things that allows you to do something very difficult. Take that away and suddenly the scale of the job can become paralysing. In front of a more negative backdrop, young conductors can lose their biggest asset, namely the confidence that knows no alternative. Of course, young musicians have a great deal to learn from those more experienced, but there's a lot an older generation can be reminded of by the young too. For Brearley, 'One would hesitate to back a fully adult person (should one exist) in any serious contest. There is nothing like a sudden upsurge of maturity to impair the will to win.' Experience isn't always an upward curve. It unquestionably makes you a better musician but that might be irrelevant if it also tarnishes your passion, hope, and joy.

★

I used to feel nauseous before a rehearsal with an orchestra I didn't know. Even worse before some I did know. It's hard to remember exactly why. Obviously, the dynamic of leading people through their day is a little intimidating but the psychological hurdles you jump along the way are, to confuse the sporting analogies, par for the course. It is not exactly a surprising part of the job description. Nor is the responsibility to be a persuasive musician. At an amateur or student level people have opinions about your work, but these orchestras are normally fully engaged with their own challenges. Most professional environments, however, are more opinionated ones, and there are not many jobs that expose you quite so personally as conducting does. For private people, who still want to share the musical part of their personality with others, to be thrust into a situation in which you know you are being constantly assessed can be inhibiting.

As you get older you realise that nerves can be a positive force. I would not say I am less nervous now but experience has taught me to compartmentalise my feelings, and that bottling them up can simply suggest a diffidence that is not a fair presentation of how I feel. Destructive nerves come from knowing you are doing something you are not really meant to be doing, but if you trust yourself and truly believe that the reasons you want to conduct are sincere and worthwhile, you can channel your adrenalin into an energy that enables you to achieve more than you would without it. What you cannot afford to do is lose your nerve. No conductor has ever died because an orchestra didn't enjoy a rehearsal, and there is nothing dangerous about what you do unless you attach value to your reputation. In any event, your reputation will best be served by a desire to do well, not a fear of doing badly.

We are often encouraged to do something as if it were for the first time, acknowledging that fear of failure is brought on by experience. But I am not sure that the first time one does something it is especially good. We just don't have anything to compare it with. Experience can be a positive influence. Far better to conduct as if you will never do so again. That forces your care to be about a present that is enriched by the past not inhibited by the future. There is great merit in the perspective that comes from a 'what-the-hell' approach.

Most of us have as a core a metaphorical pillar the various levels of which alternate between confidence and insecurity. At a particular level we have no doubt about who we are. Underneath that we might not be so sure. Dig a little deeper and we are convinced, only to be once again less certain as we continue exploring downwards. And so it goes on. The only levels that really matter are the ones on the top and the bottom. Many people appear nerveless on the surface only to be riddled by a lack of self-belief. Others come across as tentative when in fact they have a rock-solid trust in their own ability. The foundation of our personality is the one that engages us most but in a profession where how you come across is all important, you have to be aware of how others perceive you too. Ideally there is no difference. It's healthier if personality and persona are not too much at odds with one another.

There is a joke that says the difference between God and a conductor is that God knows He's not a conductor. The perception that all conductors are arrogant is something I find profoundly embarrassing. To a certain extent people expect it from those in authority, maybe even feel comfortable if they can say their expectations are fulfilled by it. But there is no excuse for arrogance, and I actually don't think you can be a good conductor without feeling humility towards the music and empathy with the players. It is not arrogant to trust yourself, and you have to be able to do that if you are to do your job well. Only by having supreme confidence in your own opinions can you truly relinquish yourself to the composer and the orchestra. I would say that it is a lack of trust in yourself that easily manifests itself as a lack of trust in others, and that what is considered arrogant is often just an expression of deep-rooted insecurity.

By necessity, your confidence has to have a very public face. People feel comfortable around confident leaders. But though self-assurance is necessary for a conductor to be considered successful, it is a shame if this success starts to disconnect your personal confidence from the musical source it first sprang from. If your fame dictates your musical and personal choices, they are unlikely to be the right ones. Fame can be intoxicating but on its own it achieves nothing.

The perception of glamour that surrounds the role of the conductor is not always the reality. Beneath the surface there can be a great deal of disappointment. I could count on my fingers and toes the number of performances I have given that I am 100 per cent proud of, those in which absolutely everything seemed to go right. There are also a few that I thought bore so little resemblance to my musical wishes that I am embarrassed to recall them. Yet these memories, superlative in both directions, might not be shared by everyone who heard them. It's possible that some in an audience enjoyed the performances I judged a failure and were bored by the ones I considered outstanding. Music is in the ear of the listener and it's good to develop a gracious acceptance of people's stage-door compliments, whatever you thought of the performance yourself. Your opinion is not especially relevant. Even so, you make music for your own benefit too, and the regret surrounding what you perceive to be a disappointment can last a long time. Often even longer than a positive memory.

The same is true for reviews. The bad ones are more cause for reflection than the good.

Criticism has always been part of the classical music world. The relationship between performers and critics is symbiotic, an intriguing equilibrium hovering somewhere between wary respect and circumspect appreciation. Performers have the opportunity to move thousands. Critics can disseminate that influence to thousands more. Or not.

It is unfortunate that a critic's job description carries with it such negative connotations. But without disapproval, approval has no context. No one wants universal castigation, yet there is also something disturbing about constantly gushing superlatives. Both success and failure carry risks and perhaps it's true that the most interesting performances are those that divide the critics.

Ask most musicians if they read their reviews and they either say yes, or they say no, or they say no and mean yes. When I started conducting I read every review out of a mixture of curiosity and pride. When I began to get bad ones I disliked the power they had over me and refused to read any at all. I then realised that such an extreme response didn't diminish the critic's power but, rather, reinforced it, and that the best approach was to read them all but trust yourself to learn from the comments you accept and ignore the ones you disagree with. However, it isn't easy to look at yourself with such internal fortitude. Especially as your public reputation is not irrelevant to your opportunities to work. But though agents, PR managers, and performers themselves have no reservations about using a good press quote for promotional purposes, at the highest level of the profession those making decisions trust in their own opinions.

Most conductors know whether they have done a good performance or not, and the wider scale of other people's observations should not outweigh the value of our own personal opinions. There is plenty to gain from discovering what someone thinks of your work but, ultimately, probably more to lose. A sensitivity to the critics also affects how you interact with your fellow performers – especially in opera, where there are normally a considerable number of performances left after the reviews have been published. If any of the singers have been cruelly treated, it can be hard to know what approach to take. If you are the victim yourself, others will be apprehensive too. There is often an elephant in the room that everyone wants to handle differently. Colleagues can offer much needed confidence to one another but there are many who prefer to operate within an environment of denial in order to remain true to who they are and what they believe in. Both responses are valid.

I used to be able to tell which newspaper people read by whether or not they asked about my concert with jovial curiosity or apprehensive concern. Nowadays the internet offers an opportunity for anyone who can be bothered to read almost every review and this panorama diminishes the power of any particular one. But such ready availability makes avoiding critical opinions harder, and you eventually discover one way or another how your performance has been received. On the whole, there are always plenty of people who mention your good reviews, yet the ominous silence in the days that follow some concerts tells its own story. I remember once being about to start my second performance of an opera, proud of myself for having been strong enough to steer clear of what had been written about the first night. But it was a strength that crumpled the moment I heard the concertmaster whisper that he thought the critics had been unnecessarily harsh about me in that morning's papers.

Dealing with criticism is a small price to pay for the privilege of performing and the two have always gone hand in hand. I doubt Aristotle was being original when he said the only way to avoid criticism is to 'say nothing, do nothing, and be nothing'. Having your concerts reviewed is part and parcel of the profession and you can be thankful that your work is considered important enough for others to care. Performers might disparage those they consider to be 'eunuchs at a harem' but they would be far more upset to be ignored by them altogether.

However much one can take encouragement from there never having been a musician who hasn't been lampooned at some point by someone somewhere, negative criticism undoubtedly has an effect. 'I pay no attention to anybody's praise or blame. I simply follow my own feelings.' That's easy to say if you are Mozart. Most performers are insecure. Self-doubt is a prerequisite to discovery. But there's a difference between asking questions of yourself in private and having them answered by others in public. After a particularly bad review I sometimes try to recall this wonderful line from a nineteenth-century art critic who once wrote in *The Examiner*, 'Rembrandt is not to be compared in the painting of character with our extraordinarily gifted English artist, Mr Rippingille.' It offers valuable perspective – for at least a few minutes.

★

Those who spend their lives being paid to do what they love are lucky indeed, but the cliché that your passion and your work are the same thing is not always as simple a bliss as one might assume. People are good at music because they love it and are lucky to have a talent for it. But like most creative jobs, it is a blend of craft and inspiration. You need both to be successful. To be good enough to become and, more importantly, remain a professional musician demands hard work on a consistent basis. To connect 'hard' and 'work' with something you love is a contradiction that can be complicated to resolve and I sometimes have to look outside the confines of conducted music to maintain the purity of my musical enthusiasm.

I find it hard not to associate a work I have performed

with the experience of having done so, and the public nature of that event, however positive, can complicate the innocence of my private connection to the music. So I am grateful that there is a whole genre of music that I will never conduct. For me, the magical world of chamber music can remain unaffected by the knowledge that comes from an intricate involvement with the practical requirements of an orchestral piece. The pleasure I get from music that I will never need to analyse, prepare, rehearse, and perform refreshes my love for what music can do.

I have often felt composers are at their most inspired when writing chamber music. Apart from those who have not composed any significant chamber pieces at all, the greatest works by the greatest composers seem to be those that need the fewest number of people to perform them. If I could listen to only one piece by Beethoven, it would be a string quartet; if it was Brahms, I would choose a violin sonata; Schubert, a piano trio; Schumann, a song. Twentieth-century composers such as Bartók, Shostakovich, and Debussy also seem to me at their most profound when not engaging in the larger-scale practicalities of a concerto, symphony, ballet, oratorio, or opera. The essence of chamber music is that, in principle at least, it is written to be played rather than listened to. Despite its frequent technical difficulties, it is intended as much for amateurs as it is for professionals. Philosophically speaking, it makes no distinction between the two. It is an active experience that equalises all those involved in its 'performance'. It does not need an audience to hear it, nor to fund it.

Orchestral music, however, is meant to be listened to.

It can only ever be rather a grand occasion. In the overall scheme of things orchestral concerts are a very recent phenomenon. There has been music for tens of thousands of years – it is older than agriculture – but only in some societies, and for merely a few centuries at most, are people asked to go and sit in a room and listen to it passively. The Western classical orchestral tradition is slim and brief across both time and place and in historical terms even to call it a tradition is quite a conceit. It certainly amounts to only a small proportion of what we know to be 'world music'. The challenges that many organisations currently face make you wonder if the orchestral experience might prove to have been just a passing fad, barely a semi-quaver in the cultural history of the human race.

A complacency that the orchestral world is too big to fail would only hasten its demise. Nor is it that big, anyway. In the crudest of terms there are perhaps only around three hundred well-known full-time professional orchestras. Even if each one employed a hundred musicians, that is a workforce roughly thirty thousand strong. Thirty thousand – in the whole world. Starbucks alone employs almost ten times that number of people. There are many hundreds of thousands who go to orchestral concerts, and an optimistic number of orchestras can report increasing ticket sales. But the success stories belong to those who, both in what and in how they play, activate their audience, and in doing so prove themselves to be indispensable to their wider community as a whole.

All of us involved have to take responsibility for making sure that people realise what orchestral music can offer before it is too late, and conductors are in a position to shoulder that responsibility more than most. We choose the music, and we set the standard for how it is performed. Orchestras can play well without conductors and they can play badly with them, but I believe that even the greatest orchestras in the world need a conductor to turn something memorable into something never to be forgotten. And unless that happens, audiences might not remember to come back. That is why conductors matter.

We need orchestral music. We need the shared experience that it offers us. In the absence of us all sitting round the campfire playing bone flutes, we need our communities to be made stronger by the profound connection that comes through the emotional expression of organised sound. Music is a civilising force, a celebration of the social cohesion needed to play and listen to it, a social cohesion that it is dangerous to think can be effective on a digital level alone.

Superficially, our world has never been so connected, yet the high degree of global disconnect is palpable. The dis-ease that comes from this contradiction creates a tension that seems likely to explode at any moment. We can connect with billions of people without leaving our home, yet though it might be comforting to be 'linked in', we know that a virtual bond cannot be trusted to protect us when we need a real one. It might be easy to 'friend' someone, even easier to 'unfriend' them, but humans have not survived so long by embracing an easy life. Our species has always been rewarded by seeking out challenges and solving them. Classical music offers just such a reward for those who know that meeting its challenges will enrich their lives. Classical music is not easy. It is not easy to write it, organise it, play it, or listen to it. We should not pretend otherwise. But I do not know what else unites the emotional, cerebral, physical, spiritual, and social qualities of a human being as much as music. Other than love and life itself.

In orchestral situations conductors are charged with inspiring these connections. You might not always succeed but when you do the sense of having been useful is profoundly gratifying. The hard work, the stress, the self-criticism, and the doubt that comes from knowing that there are many who do not even believe the role should exist is finally worthwhile. More than worthwhile.

Art asks questions of us. Some answer truthfully, even though the implications can occasionally be painful. Some lie, and to varying degrees get away with it. Some refuse to respond at all. You can think you have no choice in the matter, that how you respond is simply a question of who you are. But there is always a choice. And knowing that is the precursor to making the right choice. If conducting is a reflection of who you are, then clearly who you are matters a great deal to your conducting. But if you form your character on the basis of your conducting then who are you when you are not conducting? 'You are the music/While the music lasts,' writes T. S. Eliot in his *Four Quartets*. But what does that mean when it no longer does?

We all need an emotional hinterland that offers inspiration when we make music as well as somewhere to retreat to when we do not. Such perspective serves the intensity well. In a nutshell, conducting is about knowing what is important and what is not – and that is a question that most people face on a daily basis. In that sense, though the circumstances might be uncommon, conducting is a rather normal profession.

I imagine most people think their job is normal. Unusual is what other people do. But as ordinary as it seems to me, I am deeply conscious of how privileged conducting is on so many levels. I might have dwelled in this book on the challenges conductors face in their lives because therein lie some of the answers to those who question the what, the how, and the why of the profession itself, but if you are prepared to meet those challenges, what the experience gives you in return far exceeds the effort you put in. Every job has its Kiplingesque share of triumphs and disasters and we all try to keep a perspective on how they relate to each other. But for the lucky the positive outweighs the negative. A conductor is indeed profoundly lucky. To remember that is to be able to give fully of yourself while remaining deeply respectful of others. It is that balance that is the source of whatever you may achieve.

Being in the middle of a symphonic or operatic performance is to be surrounded by an extraordinary combination of heart and mind, body and soul. To hear some of the greatest achievements of Western culture from the closest imaginable position, exactly in the manner in which you think they should sound, played by an orchestra whose collective experience and talent must be among the widest and most breathtaking of any large group of people, and listened to by an audience that has come together to take part in a memorable and significant communal event is fortunate beyond description. At its best, shaping the invisible feels magical, but at the same time very, very real.

Acknowledgements

I am very fortunate to have grown up in a musical home. We all played the piano, and the normality of music around the house was a reassuring bedrock for personal expression. My family has never questioned my desire to conduct and a tolerance of the consequences of some of the job's pressures and responsibilities is one of many things that I will always be grateful to them for. And the fact that both my mother and my father are professional writers will have inspired this book significantly. A love for words and music is a combination I am proud to have inherited from them.

My parents had an instinct that as a child I'd benefit from being exposed to some professional musical guidance and I would regularly play my early piano pieces to Ward Swingle, a family friend and founder of the legendary Swingle Singers. I vividly recall his mellow chocolate voice calmly pronouncing one day that I should take up conducting. At the time I took this as a compliment, though with hindsight I suspect it might have been more an acknowledgement of my limitations as a pianist! Ward could tell that I was interested in music rather than in my playing of it, and to receive such advice from a musician who could count Boulez, Berio, and Bernstein among his colleagues was significant indeed.

He steered me without any suggestion of criticism – that in itself an ideal first lesson in conducting.

In a more structured sense I had three conducting teachers: George Hurst, Colin Metters, and John Carewe. They were as contrasting as chalk, cheese, and chess, but the contradictions were provocative rather than confusing and I think being forced to find my own way of resolving the differences in their musical, physical, and psychological approaches was a very good thing. I am more indebted to all three of them than I imagine they realise.

The most profound musical influence on me though was not a conductor but the Hungarian pianist György Sebők, whose path I briefly crossed at the chamber music masterclasses he led every summer in the Swiss Alps. His thoughts on music, and the sort of relationship he encouraged musicians to have with it, have shaped many of the ideas I have had over the years.

In fact I am not sure I believe there is such a thing as a truly original idea. At least if there is I don't think I've ever had one. Much of what I have written about human evolution, how our brains respond to music, and what function music should fulfil in society has been triggered by books I have read by Oliver Sacks (*Musicophilia*), Daniel Levitin (*This is Your Brain on Music*), and Philip Ball (*The Music Instinct*). Those one step removed from the goldfish bowl of musical performance seem to have a very clear grasp of what its challenges and purposes are. *The Gilded Stage* by Daniel Snowman and *A History of Opera* by Carolyn Abbate and Roger Parker are both marvellous investigations into the essence of opera.

Acknowledgements

Conducting is a lot easier to write about than to do and I have endless gratitude to the orchestra musicians, singers, and soloists whose talent, experience, patience, commitment, and trust have always given me so much to aspire to. I continue to learn from everyone I make music with and am deeply conscious of what a privileged existence that is.

Writing has made me aware how comforting it is to work with musicians who effectively carry the can for all of my musical opinions. They act as a sieve that prevents the most serious of miscalculations from ever being heard and without such protection I have felt far more vulnerable putting pen to paper than I ever have as a conductor. Yet with Faber and Faber I discovered a safety net of equal value. To have my hand held by the custodians of T. S. Eliot and Benjamin Britten is an exceptional honour that I have never taken for granted. Thank you to Belinda Matthews and Jill Burrows for conducting me through the writing process with such expertise and encouragement. I would also like to thank Martin Cullingford, editor of *Gramophone*, who, by allowing me to contribute an occasional blog to the magazine's website, provided an invaluable launchpad for this more involved version of *Shaping the Invisible*.

In draft form this book was read by Jennifer Woodside, Toby Purser, and Isla Mundell-Perkins. I cannot do justice to how much I appreciate their exceptional intelligence, care, and sincerity, and for the comfort that came from being able to trust them all so completely. Without doubt this book is immeasurably better because of the many, many improvements all three of them suggested.

Above all I thank my wife Annemieke Milks. Her knowledge, passion, and honesty as both a professional musician and now an archaeologist have enabled me to express myself with greater clarity than I could ever have done on my own. More importantly, she has always offered me the unconditional support that performers need if they are to be able to give of themselves as openly and freely as possible. Hers is a support that is never afraid to challenge, and by celebrating success while still respecting failure, she allows the reality of life to hover somewhere between the two. I would not want to do what I do or be who I am without her.